An Teallach

THE FORGE

An Teallach

THE FORGE

LESLEY TIMINGS

with

GEOFFREY COVELL

Typeset and published by **footprints** of Abernyte & Inverasdale, 2010

ISBN: 978-0-9530069-3-9

Printed by Wm Culross & Son Ltd
Queen Street, Coupar Angus
Perthshire PH13 9DF

telephone: 01828 627266
email: admin@culross.co.uk

frontispiece & cover: *An Teallach from the west, December sunrise*

CONTENTS

overleaf: *An Teallach's peaks seen from beside A832 near Dundonnell*

CONTENTS

For all those with whom we have walked, talked, camped, climbed and shared time in the mountains

ACKNOWLEDGEMENTS

With thanks to our friends who have supported the journeys on foot and in mind that have contributed to this book, especially to Moira Burks and Lorna Rylance, and to Sue Fenton of **footprints**.

With gratitude to the artists and writers who have prompted our thinking and to the rock, history and landscape of An Teallach on which those thoughts have rested.

Photographs were all taken using a handheld Minolta SRT 101 given to Lesley by her father, with 28 mm, 50 mm and 135 mm lenses and Kodak slide film.

1 INTRODUCTION

Glas Mheall Mor   *Corrag Bhuidhe and Sgurr Fiona*

Loch Toll an Lochain   *The Smiddy (Scottish Mountaineering Club hut, Dundonnell)*

Southern wall of Glas Tholl   *Torridonian sandstone, Coir' a' Mhuilinn*

facing page: *An Teallach from the west (March)*

overleaf: *Toll an Lochain*

INTRODUCTION

On the northwest coast of Scotland, rising directly from the sea and reaching 1,062 metres, is a mountain with a jagged profile whose name in Gaelic means *the forge*. This is An Teallach, its five kilometre skyline unmistakable, even from far away on the few roads that skirt and cross the Scottish mainland in the vicinity of longitude five degrees west and latitude fifty-eight degrees north.

Why write a book about it? Perhaps because its pinnacles, corries, edges and crags have etched a place in the minds of mountaineers, and in the light of dawn or dusk its rose and silver rock is a favourite with photographers. Perhaps because it is thought by many to be the finest mountain on this part of the planet. Yes, all of these; and because An Teallach has a wildness that draws the spirit, prompting questions about understanding and context, not only of the mountain but of human beings in its company.

An Teallach has eleven individual peaks over 3,000 feet (914 metres) – that historic figure by which Scottish mountains are classified – and long rounded shoulders which further extend the upland terrain. Its central spine, with narrow turreted crest, precipitous sides and airy buttresses, is one of the most spectacular mountain ridges in Scotland, ranked alongside Aonach Eagach in Glencoe, the Carn Mor Dearg arête adjacent to Ben Nevis, the great ridge of the Cuillin on Skye and the summit traverses of two of its close neighbours in the northwest, Liathach and Beinn Eighe.

Ridges and rock are essential elements of An Teallach's character but what defines the mountain's grandeur is its richly sculpted form and superb setting, with roots plunged into the waters of loch and sea, in a dazzling landscape of indented coastline, islands, glens and fellow hills.

"An Teallach is an awesome, pinnacled wedge of old red sandstone regarded by many as the finest peak in Scotland."

Ralph Storer, mountaineer
100 Best Routes in Scottish Mountains
(1987)

Below the highest points, Bidein a' Ghlas Thuill and Sgurr Fiona, are two deeply cut corries side by side, carved from Torridonian sandstone with headwalls of band upon band of lined and fractured faces, topped by the peaks. The larger corrie has enclosing ridges capped by Cambrian quartzite and the most impressive features of the mountain's scenery: a small loch wrapped in a semicircle of crags 500 metres high with a crown of irregular spikes and towers. These east-facing corries are not alone in shaping the mountain for there are five others on its western and northern sides, creating an ample stage for wind, rain and snow.

An Teallach is neither the highest nor the remotest mountain of the northwest Highlands, yet it has clear identity, standing as a single massif with just one outlier, Sail Mhor. Steep walls drop to the sea along Little Loch Broom at the mountain's northeastern margin and slopes fall almost as far on the west to the freshwater of Loch na Sealga. The wide base of Strath na Sealga separates An Teallach from other high ground in Fisherfield, Letterewe and Kinlochewe and its eastern bound is created by geology, as the underlying rock changes to Moine schists in a rolling plateau spread with bog and heather.

An Teallach's central east ridge: Bidein a' Ghas Thuill to Glas Meall Liath (right)

Pinnacles on An Teallach's main ridge: Corrag Bhuidhe and Lord Berkeley's Seat (right)

Lord Berkeley's Seat from below Corrag Bhuidhe

Here is a giant lying on the periphery of the land mass, overseeing low peninsulas dotted with habitation, backed by strath, loch and moorland, with the sea filling its north and west horizons and coming close to its side. From its tops there are glimpses of Scotland's outer isles at almost the limit of visibility across the sparkling water of the Minch. Beyond them, the continental shelf stretches for a further three hundred kilometres then ends abruptly as the sea bed falls to become the floor of the deep ocean. An Teallach is the largest landmark on this northwest edge of Europe facing the Atlantic.

The book is not only about the mountain as a physical form, it is an enquiry into An Teallach's connection with human experience. The mountain is more than rocks, ridges and summit; it carries an environment of plant and animal life, has history and place in its landscape and is party to a long relationship with human beings, from shoreline, woodlands and grazing, to peaks and buttresses.

For hillwalkers and mountaineers, the sense of scale, severity and rugged atmosphere that combine in An Teallach have made it famous, inspiring people to climb and attracting pioneers on rock and ice.

"The yearning to explore hills was born in myself in 1934, when I, a confirmed pavement-dweller, overheard a mountaineer describe a weekend visit to An Teallach in Ross-shire. He spoke of a long thin ridge, three thousand feet up, with towers and pinnacles and tall cliffs on either flank, which fell to deep corries. And from these corries clouds would boil up like steam from a cauldron, and from time to time shafts would open through them to reveal vistas of low valleys and seas and distant islands."

Looking west to An Teallach across Loch Ewe and the coastal landscape of Wester Ross

These are the words of W. H. Murray in *Undiscovered Scotland* (1951), written at a time when interest in mountaineering was growing rapidly in Britain. There were still relatively few active enthusiasts but popular imagination was caught by major expeditions and it was two years prior to Hillary and Tenzing's successful ascent of Everest. The description of An Teallach remained in Murray's memory for more than fifteen years as he grew to become a leading climber, travelling widely before seeking out the mountain of his inspiration.

For those who have never seen An Teallach, perhaps the best introduction is to drive northwest from Inverness on the A835, over the Dirrie Mor from Garve and turn west on the A832 at Braemore Junction. Sight of the distinctive skyline appears through the surrounding hills of Wester Ross and once on the A832, the Fannaichs give an intimation of the size of the mountains in this corner of Scotland. They are high and spacious with

graceful curves of ridges but their shapes do not prepare the traveller for the first full view of An Teallach. As the ribbon of road turns to cross the moor, the mountain's eastern aspect is straight ahead: six peaks along its ragged top, three huge spurs and the pair of corries gouged from the hill like eye sockets, their exposed rock sinking into shadows beneath a gallery of pinnacles. An Teallach looks big, yet is thirteen kilometres away.

An Teallach is 72 kilometres (45 miles) northwest of Inverness

An Teallach's eastern profile

"... seen from a Fannaich peak there is perhaps no mountain to compare with it in Britain. Growing from a sea of plain moorland, it becomes a multi-ridged massif in the shape of a three pronged fork, one ridge weathered into fantastic pinnacles. It is mesmerising ..."

Mike Cawthorne, long distance walker and mountaineer (2000)

The road goes directly towards the mountain and the view enlarges with stacked and angled crags in the southernmost corrie, Toll an Lochain, becoming clearer, outlined in winter with longstanding ribs of old snow. Then the descent towards Dundonnell begins, beside a fast flowing burn golden in spate and birches cream yellow in autumn; it turns through a bend and the view emerges again. The horizon has shifted upwards and space where the sky was moments before is filled by the serrated tops of An Teallach's ridges, above a thousand metres of steepening slopes in which sits the second corrie, Glas Tholl, with a foreground of weather-scoured sandstone. This is the closest

view of the mountain from a public road and the visual impact is enormous, even though the summit, on the corrie rim, is still four and a half kilometres distant.

First sight of a mountain or its image, in the same way as hearing a few words of description, can bring the first signs of attraction and commitment to climbing it. The earliest cartographic record of An Teallach appears on Timothy Pont's sketch maps made in the 1590s, drawn as a hill with a zigzag top and called *Ptalloch*. Pont was from Holland and although he never climbed An Teallach, his pen gave others the chance to feed their imaginations, and his representation of the Gaelic spoken word provides written evidence of the mountain's name.

An Teallach can mean both *the anvil* and *the forge* and there is an old smithy at its foot by the roadside in Dundonnell, now converted into a Scottish Mountaineering Club hut, *The Smiddy*. No one knows whether the mountain's name was originally associated with the presence of a forge or was chosen to portray An Teallach's character and weather conditions. When the forge is working, as water cools hot metal, steam swirls through the air and hides both anvil and smith. Similar turbulence of clouds over peaks and corries is a constant theme in later writing about the mountain.

Thomas Pennant, a Welshman, toured northwest Scotland in 1772 and published an account of his travels, coloured with extravagant descriptions of scenery and a mixture of fear and awe through which mountainous areas were perceived at his time. From an anchorage in Little Loch Broom, he wrote of a hill called *Tallochessie* that '*may vie with the highest I have seen.*' He was able to catch sight of the crags and ridges of An Teallach

and had been told their names by his hosts in Dundonnell.

"A chain of rocky mountains ... with sides deep, dark and precipitous; with summits broken, sharp, serrated, and spiring into all terrific forms; with snowy glaciers lodged in the deep shaded apertures. These crags are called squrfein, or 'hills of the wind'; they rather merit the title of squrshain, or 'rocks of wind' ..."

Thomas Pennant, topographer and naturalist
A Tour in Scotland and Voyage to the Hebrides 1772

Over one hundred and fifty years later, Scottish writer and naturalist Seton Gordon captured the winter atmosphere of An Teallach in words that come closer to the experience that many present day visitors might want to remember.

Glas Tholl, the northerly of An Teallach's two east-facing corries, seen from beside the A832

Corrag Bhuidhe

"Gathering clouds hid the sun, and from An Teallach rose vaporous mists like smoke from some giant forge. A wandering whirlwind caught up a column of frozen snow and carried it over the hillside just beneath me. The breath of the north wind was keen. Across the snow led the track of a fox. A golden eagle sailed across the hill in the teeth of the breeze, a dark, determined form."

Seton Gordon (1935)

Mountaineers are transient and recent travellers on An Teallach. For much of the ten millennia since the Highlands emerged from ice ages, humans with other purposes have walked on their ground: first nomads then generations of those who made their homes in the glens and on loch and sea shores. When a hand is laid on An Teallach's Torridonian sandstone it touches the fabric of the mountain that was made millions of years ago and remoulded by ice. In the same way, present visitors can reach towards people who spent their lives close to An Teallach in the more recent past through the names of its features, recorded in their words. Gaelic is An Teallach's language, spoken for fifteen hundred years around these slopes (originally spreading from Ireland to replace an older Pictish tongue), surviving Norse influences and still heard here until the second half of the twentieth century. It was local Gaelic names that early mapmakers recorded

Coir' a' Ghiubhsachain, corrie of the fir forest

18

as they worked on surveys of the northwest, handing them down from map to map and eventually to the editions now used by walkers.

Simon Schama and James Hunter, both historians, write from a perspective that is alive to landscape and human presence, giving credence to the experience of being at a particular location and expressing thoughts and feelings drawn from that place which relate to its past. Schama calls it *'the archive of the feet'* (1996), and Hunter defines it as *'that feeling for location which is only to be obtained by spending time in, and responding to, the places about which one writes'* (1999). For mountaineers and hillwalkers, the converse of this message would urge them to take time to appreciate and respond to the human legacy of the landscape within which their quests for summits, rocks and ridges are set.

Mountains rarely have history written on their slopes, nor in mountaineering guides. In the first four chapters of this book, An Teallach's past is explored through its seasons, weaving together threads of the natural environment with human connections, and following the leads that Gaelic placenames provide. As symbols and subjects of achievement, mountains are a human creation and inheritance, separate from other strands of their history in geological time or through climatic change. They can be personal and evocative, in addition to being known as landmark features of a locality, with links to its community, both present and long gone. The impression made by a mountain of the scope and scale of An Teallach on a human being is individual and subjective. It depends on inward

Coire Mòr an Teallaich: upland grazing on north-facing slopes below the mountain's summit

state, knowledge and understanding of the mountain, who the person is and how they are feeling; and on outward attention, focus of the senses and acuteness of observation. Although much of a day on the mountain will be rooted in the present, an awareness of An Teallach's history can be the foundation of a richer experience, responding to live moments.

As each person chooses where and when to walk or climb on An Teallach, they are creating openings for their senses and providing a canvas for their inward state. Later chapters of the book lay out a series of routes, taking the reader by the hand, suggesting the nature of opportunities that each route gives and reflecting on the mountain's past and present. They unravel human aspirations of being in a wild, mountainous environment and dig into the depths of 'where?' as well as 'why?' in treading different paths.

Whatever preparation there has been in mind or body, it is the person themself – no more, no less – that stands on the slopes of the mountain on the day of their choice. The quality of their experience – and yours too if you go with them – is a once-only mix of what An Teallach offers on that day and what they bring with inward awareness and to outward attention. The mountain is the anvil on which the experience is forged.

Glas Meall Liath

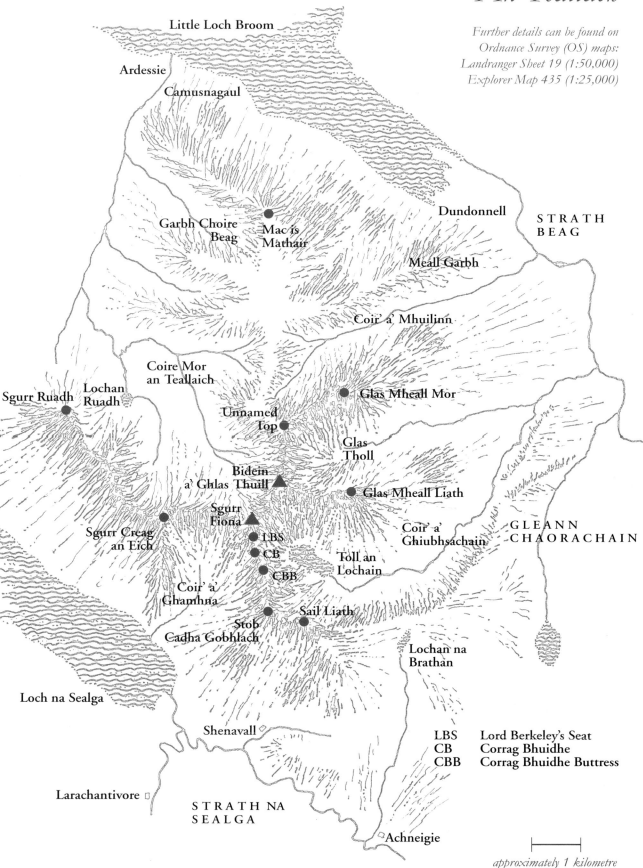

An Teallach

*Further details can be found on
Ordnance Survey (OS) maps:
Landranger Sheet 19 (1:50,000)
Explorer Map 435 (1:25,000)*

Little Loch Broom

Ardessie

Camusnagaul

Dundonnell

STRATH
BEAG

Garbh Choire
Beag

Mac is
Mathair

Meall Garbh

Coir' a' Mhuilinn

Coire Mor
an Teallaich

Glas Mheall Mor

Sgurr Ruadh

Lochan
Ruadh

Unnamed
Top

Glas
Tholl

Bidein
a' Ghlas Thuill

Glas Mheall Liath

Sgurr
Fiona

Coir' a'
Ghiubhsachain

GLEANN
CHAORACHAIN

Sgurr Creag
an Eich

LBS

CB

CBB

Toll an
Lochain

Coir' a'
Ghamhna

Sail Liath

Stob
Cadha Gobhlach

Lochan na
Brathan

Loch na Sealga

Shenavall

LBS   Lord Berkeley's Seat
CB   Corrag Bhuidhe
CBB   Corrag Bhuidhe Buttress

Larachantivore

STRATH NA
SEALGA

Achneigie

approximately 1 kilometre

2   WINTER

Coir' a' Ghiubhsachain   Ridgetop north of Sron a' Choire

Rhododendron by Garbh Allt   Slopes of Coire Mor an Teallaich

Shadows of An Teallach's peaks,   Torridonian sandstone on lower slopes of
  Coire Mor an Teallaich   Sail Liath

                  facing page: An Teallach from the west (February)

                     overleaf: Gullies in Glas Tholl

WINTER

As the shortest day lightens, clouds are still tinged with crimson at half-past nine. The sun is low in the sky, far to the south of east, striking the rims of An Teallach's two great corries and casting long shadows. North of Bidein a' Ghlas Thuill on the ridgetop plateau between Coir' a' Mhuilinn and Coire Mor an Teallaich, the undulations of soil creep terraces are accentuated into bold stripes.

Signs of life are muted and bright colours are rare: a spot of lime green lichen to catch the eye and a sparkle of sunlight on damp red leaves of bog myrtle, fallen in autumn. An Teallach's sculptural form is cloaked in shades of grey and brown set against sea and lochs in steely blue and green, ruffled by wind. On the crags of Glas Tholl, gleaming black rock is intermingled with matt whiteness of snow, creating irregular patches and patterns. As the year draws to a close the dormancy of life is all around and it is air and water that make the greatest impact.

The climate of the northwest Highlands is oceanic and the wettest months are October, December and January. The fierceness of winter manifests itself in rain and sleet, driven by westerly gales, with occasional spells of calm. As he waited for a fine cold day for his ascent of An Teallach, W. H. Murray described the weather as '*grey and lowering clouds, the occasional drizzle of sleet, the raw damp wind*' (1951).

For mountaineers it seems as if size of slope or peak becomes larger as length of days shorten. There are few people even on well-trodden tracks, yet a freezing February weekend brings out a crowd of visitors to the mountain. The traverse of An Teallach's ridges under full snow cover is an experience to be savoured, packing

into precious hours of daylight the best of the season's tastes and sights.

Although human beings clothe themselves well for a day of winter mountaineering, part of what is relished is the bite of the weather, touching heart and mind as much as face and hands. Being in the midst of icy air or swirling snow can be exhilarating, and the physical demands of climbing in cold conditions are rewarded with the splendour of winter scenery.

"Another big day, enough for a lifetime. The rocks, the air, everything speaking with audible voice or silent; joyful, wonderful, enchanting, banishing weariness and sense of time. No longing for anything now or hereafter as we go home into the mountain's heart."

John Muir, naturalist and conservationist (1911)

Awareness of vulnerability is raised in harsh mountain weather as human beings are belittled by the austerity of the environment. Nonetheless, taking time to pause is possible. Amongst the bleakness of the mountain, from cold wet rock to dark silhouettes on a far horizon, winter stillness is a fine balance between the need for movement as a drive of survival and the luxury of absorbing the atmosphere of the season. Keeping still, observing spectacular natural surroundings and holding the mind in quietness are different challenges from climbing to a summit, with different delight.

Human and animal voices are scarce at this time of year but wind and water are audible. Gales drum the air over open spaces and against the mountain, thrashing An Teallach's woodlands. During calmer days, leaves on Scots pine and rhododendron rustle as moisture drips between them, and the slopes hold sounds of swift-flowing burns.

On the mountain there are only minimal indications of modern life, speed being the most obvious – a fast moving car, boat or plane – seen peripherally and in contrast to unmoving rock, which is at the centre of the winter landscape. An Teallach's rosy pink Torridonian sandstone is 800 to 1000 million years old, layered horizontally, weathered into terraces, cut by vertical joints and rounded by centuries of wind, water and ice into curvaceous towers. The tops of Sail Liath and Glas Mheall Liath carry a pale grey layer of later quartzite, looking much like a recent fall of snow. Yet ice crystals, rock and life-forms have equally ancient heredity, constructed with atoms and energy that have been part of the universe from time before the mountain and its planet even existed.

"All of the rocky and metallic material we stand on, the iron in our blood, the calcium in our teeth, the carbon in our genes were produced billions of years ago in the interior of a red giant star. We are made of star stuff."

Carl Sagan, astronomer and educator (1973)

An Teallach's shape comes from repeated glaciation. The last ice age was at its height 18,000 years ago when Scotland's mountains were hidden below an ice cap that stretched from beyond the Hebrides across the North Sea to Norway. Emptying the contents of An Teallach's two immense corries is typical of movement of rock by ice as the largest glaciers in the northwest slowly ground their way east. Smaller glaciers tugged at the northern and western edges of An Teallach, scooping out its other five corries. The structure that remains is steep-sided, with high narrow arêtes, smooth-sloped lower tops and sweeping hollows.

Approaching Toll an Lochain on Torridonian sandstone slabs

Toll an Lochain

The human emptiness of the views and paucity of vegetation are testimony to the history of the last few hundred years. Where there is now a remote and vast space for thought in the majesty of winter, there was once forest, cultivation, communities, homes and trade.

Remoteness is relative and depends upon starting points. Today, visitors to northwest Scotland may feel it to be remote – especially from their centres of life and understanding – but in earlier times it was not so. There were few visitors for pleasure but people still travelled and the Highlands were connected by culture, language, kingdoms, scholarship and way of life to other parts of the world. The sea was a mainstay of communication to places near and far, not a means of separation.

There has long been habitation close to An Teallach, as human beings have chosen to make their homes on loch-side sites like this for the last four millennia. Nomadic people made encampments for a few days or weeks then many generations later, on the shores of Little Loch Broom with An Teallach's slopes giving shelter from the westerly winter gales, they made plans to stay. Here they could continue hunting and fishing – fundamentals of their nomadic lifestyle – as well as rearing animals and growing crops, requirements of their new permanence.

For some of those past centuries the climate was milder and drier than it is today but winter was always a hard time. The nights were just as long then as now, and across the loch or down the glen, dim lights will have been seen – soft orange from a fire, yellow from an oil flame or candle – as a door was opened or window covering moved.

The communities of Dundonnell and Camusnagaul on the shore of Little Loch Broom probably hold An Teallach's longest human history. Camusnagaul means *bay of the strangers* or *lowlanders*, hinting that there were others nearby to give it that name, even before the strangers came. Amongst those who arrived to settle along the coast were Vikings, choosing places like Gruinard, in Old Norse 'grunna fjord' meaning *shallow bay*, where the water from Loch na Sealga drains into the sea. Landings by boat would have been reliable here and at Ullapool too, only a few sea miles to the north, which also owes its name to Norse settlers. Vikings came initially as plunderers towards the end of the eighth century, then made their homes here in peace in the years that followed. It is easy to see why Scandinavian people found this coastline attractive, as it is so reminiscent of their homeland with fjord-like sea lochs, mountains and a sunset into the sea in the west. Here too, the winter nights are shorter.

Timothy Pont's maps of the 1590s show many communities in glens around An Teallach, and he drew a clachan on the site of the present bothy, Shenavall, at the mountain's southern foot. Clachans were where most people lived in the Highlands at that time, each a group of ten or so simple family houses forming a township, with byres, stabling for cattle and horses close by and shared land for cultivation and hill pasture. This was the life that was led below Sail Liath, where today the bothy provides welcome shelter on a winter night.

A century after Pont, the poet James Hogg visited Strath na Sealga and wrote that it was inhabited only by shepherds. Clearance of the land for sheep had begun, and with it, removal of clusters of communal living in the glens of this part of Wester Ross.

At the eastern foot of Beinn Dearg Mor, An Teallach's mountain neighbour across Strath na Sealga, there was a lodging house known by the name Larachantivore, *site of the big house,* used by geologists and surveyors in the late nineteenth century. From the warmth of its fireside or lee of the building, residents and travellers alike had an extensive view of the southwest profile of An Teallach. 'Larach' means *ruin* as well as *site*, giving a sign of the ups and downs of Larachantivore as a place of human dwelling, where today a stalker's cottage and estate lodge continue that thread, although with only occasional occupants.

A couple of kilometres southeast from Shenavall is the solitary house of Achneigie. When W. H. Murray came to An Teallach in February 1950, Shenavall had been empty for ten years but Achneigie was home to the Urquart family. Murray and his two friends knocked at the door, were made welcome and invited inside where they met another resident, the schoolmistress, there to teach the three Urquart children. Murray wrote:

"We were surprised to hear cattle in the byre and see a bright light in the house. For I would not have believed that in winter people could have been found to live here. The only links with civilisation are the hill track to Dundonnell or a ten mile track west to Gruinard Bay. There is no other occupied house in the glen."

W. H. Murray, mountaineer
Undiscovered Scotland (1951)

The upland of An Teallach has no signs of permanent habitation and no long history of human presence to match that of the coast and glens. Nonetheless, perhaps the nomadic people of 7,000 to 4,000 BC ventured upwards on the wooded slopes of the mountain, driven by human curiosity or a wish to see further afield. They ate fish caught by line and hook, meat from wild animals (snared, trapped or speared) and berries, roots, leaves and nuts from the woods. The mountain will have been a familiar part of their homeland, around which they lived, travelling by foot or boat between places with different sources of food. It is possible that they were the first explorers of An Teallach's tops. They left few traces and the nearest archeological evidence of their presence has been found on the shoreline at Shieldaig and Red Point, about fifty kilometres from the mountain. Although their history on higher ground is invisible, it is one in whose footsteps present day hillwalkers follow, coming with the seasons, less often in winter, more in summer.

Likewise there are no records of people who have lived permanently in the shadow of An Teallach being pioneers in ascent of its peaks. The only local reason for going to the high slopes was their use for summer grazing, which may have given an adventurous shepherd

An Teallach from near Gruinard

the opportunity to climb – unknown and unacknowledged – to the summit. Domestic cattle and sheep were always brought to lower ground in autumn, as they still are, so there were no people on the mountain in winter. Those who go there now for recreation are a new tradition in An Teallach's history.

Before the eighteenth century, mountains were seen as difficult places to travel, gloomy and threatening, both in terms of terrain and inhabitants (if any). They were thought to be bad enough in summer and unthinkable in winter: perspectives formed from viewpoints far away and in comparison with lowland Scotland or England. Encounters with the Highlands were reported in extremes, as by Thomas Pennant, in describing An Teallach and its surroundings:

"... vast mountains, naked, rugged and dreary, their bases sloping furrowed with long clefts, emptying their precipitated waters into the river beneath."

Thomas Pennant, topographer and naturalist
A Tour in Scotland and Voyage to the Hebrides,
1772

Others who ventured to the Highlands at this time were, like Pennant, purposeful, but not mountaineers. They were cartographers, mineral prospectors, new landowners or military men, rarely making ascents, rarely chosing to travel in winter and certainly not aspiring to gain pleasure from being amongst Scotland's mountains.

The first written record of an ascent of An Teallach is by John MacCulloch at some time between 1810 and 1824. A doctor by training, MacCulloch claimed to have climbed nearly all of Scotland's mountains, combining this with his employment as a geologist and surveyor.

Within his lifetime, travel began to become fashionable and he wrote one of the first guides to northern Scotland. Whilst he applauds other mountains for their fine views, his experience on An Teallach is recounted with apprehension and was not altogether enjoyable:

Glas Tholl

Skyline of Toll an Lochain: (left to right) Corrag Bhuidhe buttress, Corrag Bhuidhe, Lord Berkeley's Seat and Sgurr Fiona

"I proceed for some distance along the giddy ridge, in hopes of seeing its termination; but all continued vacant, desolate, silent, dazzling, and boundless."

John MacCulloch, doctor, surveyor, mountaineer
Highlands and Western Isles (1824)

A century later, John Muir might have written with joy about silence and dazzle, but Dr MacCulloch, even though an ambitious peak bagger, was touched with fear.

An Teallach has now been climbed by mountaineers for nearly two hundred years. Hugh Munro, author of *Tables giving all the Scottish mountains exceeding 3,000 feet* (1891), made the first known traverse of An Teallach's main ridge in 1893 with a group of fellow members of the Scottish Mountaineering Club. They measured heights of peaks and discovered the shape of the mountain, which had been

something of a mystery for those who came to it as visitors, although perhaps not to others whose animals grazed on its slopes every summer. Munro and his friends were first too in expressing genuine pleasure in what they found, even at their initial glimpse:

"... the glorious hills themselves, suddenly bursting through the storm clouds, black, snow-slashed, and jagged against the setting sun."

W. W. King and H. T. Munro, mountaineers
An Teallach: Ross-shire (1893)

They heralded the future of An Teallach for hillwalkers and climbers, both in winter and summer. The headwalls of Glas Tholl and Toll an Lochain are magnificently situated within the mountain to tempt rock climbers but their structure is broken into layers, loose in parts and interspersed with vegetation, making

Sail Liath (left) and Stob Cadha Gobhlach,
An Teallach's southern tops

climbing hazardous. When frozen under ice and
snow the walls are much more stable, and there
are classic lines of ascent by buttresses and
gullies over several hundred metres.

In the early years of the twentieth century
members of the Scottish Mountaineering
Club (SMC) made many trips to the northwest
Highlands including pioneering rock and ice
ascents on An Teallach. Famous climbing
partners Ling and Glover visited in 1907 and
created the first recorded climbing route on the
mountain, Corrag Bhuidhe Buttress, which the
pair described as steep grass and rock. In 1910,
another SMC partnership Sang and Morrison
completed the first winter climbing route,
Hayfork Gully, a deep cleft holding ice in the
crags of Glas Tholl.

In the decades that followed, An Teallach
established itself in the hearts of those who
came to know the Scottish mountains, their
appreciation extending to its ridges and
pinnacles, its location in the far northwest
and the grandeur of its winter mountain
environment. W. H. Murray's wait at Shenavall
for perfect weather was rewarded with a cold
clear day in which he delighted:

*"The last slope of Sail Liath was a wind-packed
snow-field, arching up to a huge silver dome. The
edge of the dome had a curve like good china, a
vast and flawless curve starting out against the blue
behind. The blue was lucid: that early morning
blue, which one associates with South Sea lagoons;
and the snow-dome's edge flowed upon it. I had seen
nothing on mountains more simple than this edge,
and nothing more beautiful."*

W. H. Murray, mountaineer (1951)

In March 1969, Tom Patey, mountaineer and
doctor from Ullapool, climbed on An Teallach
with his friend Chris Bonnington, making a
winter ascent named Checkmate Chimney in
Glas Tholl. This is a slanting groove across the
northern end of the corrie's headwall and a
characteristically bold rock and ice route.
Although an array of winter climbs has now
been established in both large corries, long-
frozen ice and snow are no longer reliable
annual occurrences. The summit and tops of
the main ridge, enjoyable still in milder weather,
are the jewels in An Teallach's crown and it is
to them that modern mountaineers continue
to head, as did the pioneers of the past. They
follow those first giddy steps taken by Dr
MacCulloch, sharing Munro's delight in jagged
peaks and hoping for more of W. H. Murray's
flawless curves of wind-packed snow. The
winter view from Bidein a' Ghlas Thuill will
always be one of the mountain's treasures.

*"I stood on the hill-top beside the ice encrusted
cairn and looked over the vast precipices to where
dark Toll an Lochain lies in the heart of this
mighty hill. Across the abyss, where the eagle soars
and the ptarmigan at times flies like a drifting
snowflake, rose the awe-inspiring turrets and
slender spire of Sgurr Fiona, just nine feet lower
than the hill-top where I stood."*

Seton Gordon, naturalist, mountaineer (1935)

Feral goats on An Teallach's lower ground by Little Loch Broom (and below)

In contrast with human visitors, many of An Teallach's animals seek shelter from the hardship of the season and come down towards the glens and sea. Herds of goats with long shaggy hair in black, brown and white – wild after many generations since the original domestic stock escaped or was abandoned – are most easily seen at this time of year. They can survive the bitterest of mountain conditions but in January and February are often along the shore of Little Loch Broom, eating gorse at the roadside. Adult billies carry large curved horns which appear above shrubs and tussocks as they feed, and nannies have small kids close at their heels, born in these winter weeks. They are agile and wary, but unhurried if disturbed, and free to roam wherever they can, with no natural predators other than man. Being voracious

previous page: *Sgurr Fiona from slopes below Bidein a' Ghlas Thuill*

eaters of any vegetation, they are culled in small numbers by local residents to safeguard trees, gardens and grazing.

Red deer are on the lower slopes too, seeking food and the protection of trees, large boulders and rock terraces. Stags and hinds live separately and move with their group, easily distinguished over winter months as stags have fully grown antlers and hinds have none. Descendants of larger deer species that inhabited the area following the last ice age, red deer have lived amongst these mountains for centuries along with other large animals, now gone: lynx, bear, wild boar and wolves. The lynx became extinct four thousand years ago but bears were known in Scotland up until the ninth or tenth century, wild boar until the sixteenth and wolves until the eighteenth. It was neither winters' severity nor lack of food that precipitated their going. All have been victims of man as a hunter, killing animals to eat, to protect livestock or as a trophy collector. Of the other deer, reindeer survived in Scotland until the twelfth century and great elk until the eighteenth.

An Teallach's slopes and corries are home to many red deer. They are shy of human beings, as might be expected from animals with such a long history of being hunted, and an annual cull (to maintain a healthy population) plus some seasonal shooting for sport are still a part of their existence. When the weather is severe, it is to An Teallach's woodland that deer come, moving quietly between the birches in Gleann Chaorachain and browsing on last season's grasses, leaves and early spring shoots.

As the year moves forward and days begin to lengthen, soon after dawn and before mountaineers have made their ascents, alone on the uppermost slopes there are ptarmigan in bold white plumage. They are as well camouflaged amongst patches of snow and rock as in their subtle mix of grey and brown in summer. Other creatures are hidden in sheltered places, awaiting the sharpness of hunger to bring them out on the mountain or the arrival of warmer days for their return from winter absence.

Deer in Gleann Chaorachain

3   SPRING

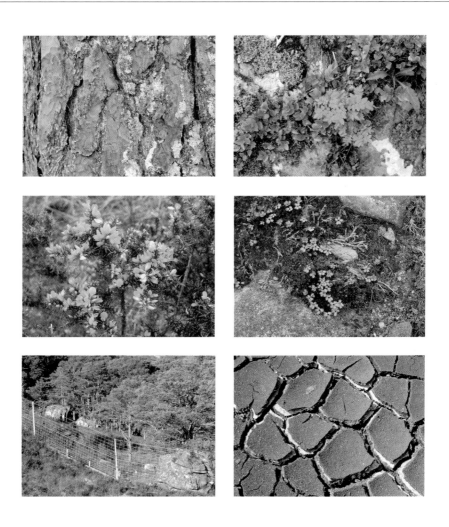

Bark on Scots pine by Garbh Allt

Gorse, Strath Beag

Scots pines below Glas Mheall Mor

facing page:

overleaf:

Rowan seedling near Allt Airdeasaidh

Moss campion, Sron a' Choire

Cracked peat, Coir' a' Ghiubhsachain

An Teallach from the west (May)

Birches on An Teallach's northern slopes
below Mac is Mathair

SPRING

Land is emerging from the grip of winter, daylight hours are lengthening rapidly and birdsong has returned to the slopes of the mountain. As March passes, there is frogspawn in small pools and dippers are busy with nests in holes, close to their territory of flowing water. At the base of An Teallach by Little Loch Broom and beside the river in Strath na Sealga, gorse bushes bear brilliant yellow flowers that have been blooming since late January. By April many birds are ready to lay eggs and the call of a cuckoo is heard across the glen near the head of Loch na Sealga.

In the woodland of Gleann Chaorachain, willow and hazel carry catkins, and nearby plantations of larch have begun their change from pale russet through shades of light olive and lime to apple green. Birches are a haze of burgundy, coloured by dense wet twigs and leaf buds, soon to be transformed into a wealth of delicate spring growth.

Deer and goats move higher on the mountain, following the progress of new shoots, whilst sheep – due to lamb and fenced into the fields of Strath Beag – wait to return to upland grazing at the end of May.

Old deep snow lying longest in the steep northeast-facing corners of the two great corries begins to melt then re-freezes at night under clear skies. Fresh snow dusts the surface lightly for a few hours and in some years larger falls come as late as the first week of June.

Receding snow and emerging growth are reminders of the transition of 10,000 years ago as ice gave way to a warmer climate in which plants, animals and humans began to live. The vegetation clinging to the sparse soil of the upper ridges of An Teallach is similar to that which first grew on the newly exposed land: low lying plants tolerant of extreme weather, the higher their habitat the more rain, snow and cloud they live amongst and the less sunshine, shelter and warmth.

Dwarf juniper is common in both Toll an Lochain and Glas Tholl and has probably been in these corries ever since the ice retreated. Gnarled branches press close to the curves of rock over which they grow, seeming to clasp hold of the ground with sinewy fingers. Each plant lives for many years, its leaves tough and strong, moving little with the wind and surviving the tread of hooves and boots.

As ice left, shrubs and trees began to colonise the mountain: larger junipers and willows then birches, rowan and aspen. It was birch that dominated the new woodland, spreading widely over the slopes of An Teallach, and it remains the most prevalent tree species today. Its hardiness is belied by dancing leaves, elegant form and fine tracery of branches through which gales pass with none of the resistance that larger trees offer.

Scots pine – *Pinus sylvestris*, the woodland pine – began to appear on An Teallach around 8,000 years ago. It was already established in Ireland and England, and over the next 3,000 years became common and took the place of birch as the predominant tree on the mountain's sides. It is not known how Scots pines arrived in this part of Scotland but they transformed An Teallach, Torridon and many surrounding glens into the northwest heartland of the Caledonian Pine Forest. Scots pines from this area spread

Remnants of snow and ice at the rim of Glas Tholl

Snow patches in May on the side of Coir' a' Mhuilinn

Dwarf juniper on the slopes of Sail Liath, Toll an Lochain

eastwards as far as the Spey and the Dee, north to Sutherland, west to Skye and the outer isles, and as far south as Rannoch Moor. Trees growing today on the lower slopes of Glas Mheall Mor are true natives, able to trace their ancestry back to the pines of 8,000 years ago in a Scottish population that has remained distinct (*Pinus sylvestris* ssp. *scotica*) amongst what is now a wide-ranging species, extending across Europe and Asia.

For many generations, pines grew well on An Teallach alongside rowan, oak, holly, hazel and birch, with alder and willow on damper soils, in a cover of woodland that reached all but the highest ridges. Then, about 5,000 years ago, the climate changed to become cooler and wetter. Flatter pieces of ground began to accumulate peat, which built up over centuries as each season's dead plant material became waterlogged and acid, together stopping its complete decomposition. An Teallach's rocks are poor at providing nutrients and with high rainfall most were washed out of its thin soil leaving peat as the main alternative growing medium. Plants that could tolerate acid continued their life cycles – moorland grasses, sedges, bog myrtle and heather – but for trees, peat was a poor substitute for the more fertile and well-drained soils of the past. Fewer trees grew to replace ones that fell or died and the woods became less dense.

For the last two and a half thousand years, the pattern of climate that is experienced today has been fairly stable and for more than half of this time fifty per cent of An Teallach was covered in woodland. Oak was found on lower seaward slopes; in Strath na Sealga, alder; and up to around 600 metres on steeper ground, Scots pine with birch at its upper edge. Above the woods rose stark corrie walls and ridges, home only to dwarf shrubs and mosses.

Scots pines on An Teallach's lower slopes, as they have been for 8,000 years

Today, the range of tree species on An Teallach is the same as all those years ago, yet tree numbers are small and cover is minimal. Destruction of woodland has happened in stages, always as a result of human action, both on An Teallach and across the whole of the Caledonian Pine Forest. A sparse nomadic population made little impact on the landscape, but once permanent settlement and cultivation began there were substantial changes. At first our ancestors made clearings for themselves and their animals, then in later centuries they used ever increasing quantities of timber for fuel, building materials and smelting iron ore. They did little or no replanting and slopes cleared of trees became extensive grazing land with the vestiges of woodland burned to reduce cover for predators, both animal and human.

Even in peat soils it is possible for trees to grow from seed, replacing old ones that have fallen, but what sounds their death knell is grazing animals that eat entire seedlings and strip small trees of new leaves. On the flanks of An Teallach that rise above Loch na Sealga, where steep slopes face south and west soaking up sunshine in lengthening days, growth of vegetation is strong. Rowan seedlings open their delicate tiny leaves amongst the shelter of heather and each is a welcome mouthful for a passing goat or deer. In recent years, for some seedlings, there has been a difference which means survival beyond a first spring, due to a high fence around the cascades of the Allt a' Ghamhna and land alongside, from near the shore of Loch na Sealga to half way up the mountain.

Inside the fence are mature birch and rowan, owing their existence to roots amongst the tumble of rocks shaped by the burn where crevices and fast flowing water protected their early years from the reach of browsing animals. Now, with present day grazers excluded – deer, goats, and from late spring, occasional sheep and cattle – a rowan seedling no longer needs an impregnable site to ensure its future as a tree.

Other exclosure fences on An Teallach are helping to recreate the wooded character of the mountain's past: in Gleann Chaorachain, through regeneration from elderly birch, alder and new planting of native species, and below Glas Mheall Mor, from the remnants of the ancient forest.

It is sad that fences will have to remain as a mountain feature for several decades, imposing boundaries on an otherwise open landscape and denying wild animals the winter shelter that trees provide. However, as deer and goat numbers are large and woodland is sparse and vulnerable, there is probably no better choice at present than to surround both older trees and new seedlings with protection.

With spring days, come more visitors, not only migrant birds but human visitors too. Rainfall in April and May is at its lowest, the air is cool and fresh making views sharp and clear, and there are calm spells of spring sunshine, ideal weather for the traverse of An Teallach. In late March on a weekday, there may be no more than three or four people on the mountain yet two months later, the total could be more than a hundred.

Seton Gordon's writing – as mountaineer, field naturalist and authority on golden eagles – finds a place in An Teallach's history between early pioneer climbers and the growth of mass interest in mountaineering after the second World War. He describes An Teallach as *'one of the most inspiring of Scottish mountains'* and his field notes transport the reader to high on a ridge, sitting beside him in the 1930s, as spring takes hold:

"... sun-warmed terraces of red sandstone on which cushions of sea thrift were stirring into life."

Seton Gordon
Highways and Byways in the West Highlands (1935)

He lamented the extinction of the osprey in the Highlands and wrote of a lochan where it used to nest not far from the outflow of Loch na Sealga, northwest of An Teallach. With many pairs having been successfully re-established in Scotland, there is now hope that ospreys will return one day to breed in this part of the northwest, where the sea thrift still flowers, and eagles still fly on the wind as Seton Gordon saw them nearly seventy-five years ago.

W. A. Poucher's description of An Teallach begins, *'This range of hills is one of the most spectacular in Scotland and vies in grandeur with that of the Torridon Peaks and the Coolins of Skye':* words that many hillwalkers of the sixties, seventies and eighties will have read in *The Scottish Peaks* (1965), together with his appreciation of the mountain's *'superb sandstone architecture'* and *'two magnificent corries.'*

More recently, praise for the mountain has not lessened. Mountaineer and broadcaster Cameron McNeish writes of An Teallach as a favourite:

"... the castellated form of An Teallach, the forge, in shape and form one of the most appealing mountains in the land."

Cameron McNeish
The Munros (1996)

facing page: *Allt a' Ghamhna, Stob Cadha Gobhlach*

Likewise Jim Crumley, who has spent much time in the Scottish hills and written with passion and concern about the Cairngorms, nonetheless has special affection for An Teallach. In *Among Mountains* (1993), he calls An Teallach *'a superstar, the mightiest mountain in the West Highlands.'*

Martin Moran, mountaineer, and the late Clarrie Pashley, photographer, both residents amongst the mountains of Wester Ross for many years, share the enthusiasm:

"The mighty forge ... with its isolated position and varied form, An Teallach has something of grace and elegance, a romantic beauty that tugs the heart strings."
                    The Magic of Wester Ross and Skye (2001)

An Teallach is capable of stirring emotions, standing apart from other mountains and being written about in superlatives. So what is it that makes a mountain so appealing? For some, An Teallach holds the challenge of a long day of activity, scrambling on narrow ridges and reaching summits, and for others it is the mountain's character which draws them: the beauty of its environment and the wildness and wilderness that it exemplifies.

Appreciation of beauty in the natural world is accepted as unquestionably good in the twenty-first century, yet within timescales of only a few lifetimes it was not so. Beauty, in all its forms, is a contextual and cultural phenomenon, as illustrated by Thomas Pennant's description of An Teallach in 1772 as *'horrible'* and *'awful.'* During the century that followed Pennant's writing, perceptions of mountainous areas shifted, notably amongst people with enough money to enjoy recreation and leisure. They came from the south, travelling to the Highlands to see peaks and glens, in what

became known as the Romantic period in English speaking Britain. Wordsworth and Coleridge were part of its beginnings, writing about nature with a sense of wonder, delight and respect for its power. Artists painted Scottish landscapes in exaggerated form (although closer to the truth for An Teallach than for other locations) with precipitous crags beside enormous waterfalls and ever-present lochs, often with a foreground of deer or Highland cattle.

"Culture is the veil through which we describe nature. The process of nature continues despite our analysis. Our analysis is a part of the process of nature."

Chris Drury, environmental artist, sculptor
(1995)

Mountains moved from being fearful dark places to be part of the mix of scenery that was thought to be uplifting and attractive. They had become beautiful. The Romantic view of rural and natural environments stood in sharp contrast to both the social conditions of Victorian Britain's crowded industrialised cities and the poverty and starvation being experienced by local people in the Highlands.

A spirit of adventure and exploration, for its own sake, was born in this same era, for those who could afford it. Using profits from mills, mines and factories, there were expeditions to remote parts of Europe, Africa and Asia to bring back plants, collect historic artwork and hunt big game; and with exploration came mountaineering, growing to become an activity and sport in its own right. Present day hillwalkers and climbers have industrialisation to thank for giving many of those pioneer mountaineers the means for their chosen pursuit. It was nearly a hundred years later when others – whose grandparents', fathers'

An Teallach's ridge: Sgurr Fiona (right), Lord Berkeley's Seat and Corrag Bhuidhe

and mothers' labour unknowingly may have supported the first mountaineers – began *their* fight to give themselves time for recreation, time to be able to appreciate beauty in nature, and to have access to moor and mountain.

What began through the perspective of the Romantics as opinions of the privileged few has moulded the way in which mountaineers now think and write about An Teallach. This relatively recent English speaking heritage in the Highlands has overlain much older roots of reverence for the natural environment from agriculture, religious belief and ancient practice in Gaelic tradition. The rising popularity of the beauty of Scotland's mountains in the nineteenth and twentieth centuries coincided with severe repression of the Gaelic language by government, harsh treatment of those who spoke it and a resulting decline in its use. By

these means the landscape was robbed of its spoken human history and the connections that language can make between present understanding of terrain and a more distant past. It is fortunate only that the mapmakers arrived before the last speakers of the Gaelic language who knew the mountains were gone, but even so, there is a fundamental gap.

Gaelic speakers had given names to An Teallach's features in language that survived from before Viking occupation, dominated for a few generations yet never lost. Both Gaelic and Norse peoples had oral traditions of poetry and story going back hundreds of years and their observation of the mountains was imaginative as well as functional, using skills in description and metaphor, noticing shape and seasonal colour. As mapmakers asked about names of crags, mountains, corries and tops, they were

Sgurr Fiona from Coire Mor an Teallaich in spring sunshine

given Gaelic words and phrases which may have been in continuous use since the sixth century, when the Gaels arrived from Ireland.

Over the last fifty years, Gaelic has finally lost its live voice amongst the mountains of Dundonnell, Letterewe, Fisherfield and Kinlochewe but has been preserved, unspoken, on all maps in current use. Here is the gap. Mountaineers and hillwalkers have representations of An Teallach with richness in names but (in most cases) have no capability to pronounce or understand them and no interpretation. The land seems foreign and cannot tell its story, leaving those who come to visit the poorer. They are unable to make a link between their present experience of the mountain and the ways in which it was known by others long ago. They do not even ask, 'Why are there no pines in Coir' a' Ghiubhsachain?'

The twin ideals of wildness and wilderness are important aspects of twenty-first century appreciation of beauty in the mountains. Wildness has wide scope and can embrace steep terrain or open country with vast skies,

wind or snow, mountains, plains or islands.
The spaces and scale of corries and ridges, the
expanses of rock and frame of lochs – sea on
one side, freshwater on the other – give An
Teallach its wildness. For many hillwalkers this
is simultaneously attractive and alien. It is a
raw and elemental kind of beauty – no softly
contoured hills, meadow flowers, hedgerows,
or tall leafy trees of more comfortable
pastoral landscapes – and it ignites a spark of
excitement. A day on An Teallach is not only
about the achievement of reaching a summit
but the sensation of being in a wild place.

Views from the mountain are bigger than a
cityscape and the hillwalker has more time
to absorb them. There are fewer surprises
and movements are slower than in urban
environments: clouds shifting across the sky,
birds rising in song, a deer in smooth trot over

the moorland. On high ground, there is no
shade and no limit to visibility, with the lack
of trees adding bareness and bleakness to
the mountain's beauty. The form of the land
includes curves, peaks and profiles worn by
glaciers, water and wind: shapes with strong
association to the natural world, an absence of
vertical lines and no absolute symmetries. The
sole horizontal is the far limit of the sea.

Wilderness is distinct and different from
wildness, implying that land is uninhabited,
uncultivated with no impact by human beings.
It has grown to mean a place where plants and
animals live in their own right and in natural
balance. In this century, both for An Teallach
and the rest of the British Isles, wilderness is an
illusion, as land has been inhabited for as long
as can be traced and human action is a major
contributor to its present state.

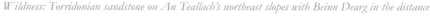

Wildness: Torridonian sandstone on An Teallach's northeast slopes with Beinn Dearg in the distance

'Last Great Wilderness': An Teallach from Loch Toll an Lochain on Beinn Dearg Mor, Fisherfield

However, in spite of the reality, the idea of wilderness has taken root amongst hillwalkers and mountaineers. The 'Last Great Wilderness' is the name given to the area from Dundonnell to Loch Maree and Kinlochewe including all of An Teallach, the Letterewe and Fisherfield mountains and extending eastwards towards the Fannaichs. From Sgurr Fiona it fills the view to the south and west, with nine Munros, including A' Mhaighdean and Ruadh Stac Mor, often described as the remotest Munros of all.

The area is scenically outstanding and one of the largest expanses of the Highlands with no public roads and almost no permanent habitation. There has been relatively little change here in the last hundred years, but nonetheless what has remained has had human influence in large measure. Whether by default or by management, the maintenance of a population of herbivores has ensured the preservation of this version of 'wilderness': open moorland and mountain with ageing trees forming small patches of woodland. The tragedy in spring is a double one as the first shoots of the season are not only important for plants, setting them up for another year of life, but also as nutritious spring food for An Teallach's wild deer and goats, to keep them healthy after winter. Both flora and fauna suffer in a habitat that has lost much of its historic balance and variety.

Fences to exclude browsing animals – not only on the slopes of An Teallach – are the most significant changes to be made to this 'wilderness' landscape in those hundred years. In itself, fencing is no closer to the ethos of wilderness than human actions of the centuries before; however, it is restorative. It looks forward to a more diverse natural environment and is in the true spirit of conservation: human intervention to keep and build upon the best from the past and not damage it for the future.

Previous generations will have seen a different spring, in a land with more forest, spoken about in a different language. Grazing animals – some, successors of theirs – now restrict the mountain vegetation, and relics of pines, felled by them or by others who came to trade, lie still in the peat. Today, the bare grandeur of An Teallach attracts mountaineers and hillwalkers who value its dramatic character, exposed rock and ridges. Before many years have passed, there may be a time when trees and woodland are again a substantial part of the mountain landscape, their beauty adding to the wildness that visitors come to be amongst.

Upland grazing in Coire Mor an Teallaich

4   SUMMER

Orchids near Allt Airdeasaidh

Birches, on the shore of Loch na Sealga

An Teallach's summit,
Bidein a' Ghlas Thuill,
from the top of Coir' a' Mhuilinn

Bog asphodel, near Allt Airdeasaidh

Gleann Chaorachain

Sgurr Creag an Eich and Loch na Sealga

facing page: An Teallach from the west (July)

overleaf: Towers below Bidein a' Ghlas Thuill
against the grey green of Glas Tholl

SUMMER

Summer is that ill-defined time between the late frosts of early June when spring flowers are in bloom while snow patches linger in the gullies and the softening light that brings August to a close with shades of purple and gold across the mountain. It is a season of greenness, at its height from Midsummer Day until the end of July.

The Gaelic speaking people of An Teallach's past used the changes marking the passage of the year to describe the backdrop to their lives. In summer, Glas Tholl and Glas Mheall Mor take on the colours of their names, *grey green hollow* and *great grey green rounded hill*. Rocks and crevices dry out, becoming paler, and ledges between them fill with vegetation, their combination making the subtle mix of the Gaelic 'glas.'

One of the finest views of Glas Tholl is from beside the A832 just before it descends to the snowgates at Corrie Hallie. Riding above foreshortened slabs on lower ground, huge concave slopes and green curves catch the sun. An upper bowl scooped from the northern corner of the corrie has more grass and less exposed rock, giving a steep route of access to the ridges above. The high point of the corrie rim in its southwest corner is Bidein a' Ghlas Thuill, *peak of the grey green hollow*, at 1,062 metres, An Teallach's summit.

In strong sunlight the upper layer of quartzite on the mountain stands out clearly as silvery grey, in Gaelic 'liath'. The central ridge from Bidein a' Ghlas Thuill extends east to Glas Mheall Liath, *grey green, pale grey rounded hill*, with quartzite cap and runs of scree reaching into the sandstone and vegetation below.

Even on the highest tops, plants are flowering: moss campion in bright magenta and alpine lady's mantle in delicate creamy green, both near the cairn on Bidein a' Ghlas Thuill. In lower damper places, butterworts have appeared like lime starfish bearing violet flowers, and in sheltered ravines there are foxgloves. Across the moorland, orchids are followed by stands of yellow bog asphodel.

By early June all the mountain birds have hatched their young, making the best of warmer weather. Amongst the rocks, ptarmigan chicks wander, tiny bundles of yellow and brown fluff the size of walnuts, with agitated parents dancing a distraction if any human beings approach.

Summer brings many visitors to the Highlands. In a short tourist season of ten or twelve weeks, travellers passing An Teallach may be not only European but American, Asian and Australian, and the road is busy with caravans, campervans, motor bikes and coaches.

For many tourists it is not extremes of wildness or wilderness that bring them here, nor is it the history of this landscape and its people, it is the scenery of northwest Scotland: the combination of coastline, islands, mountains, moors and sea.

The mountain itself has more people treading its tops and tracks as each summer passes yet most stay only for a day. By contrast, until the closing years of the eighteenth century, the few people on An Teallach's summer slopes were those whose entire lives were spent around the mountain. They were there to find food for domestic animals and thereby ensure their own survival.

An Teallach's central ridge from Bidein a' Ghlas Thuill (left) to Glas Mheall Liath, seen from the quartzite slopes of Sail Liath

On the high hills of the northwest Highlands there was a tradition (now ended) of organised and tended summer grazing not unlike the transhumance still in use in parts of the Alps and Pyrenees.

It is possible that prior to the township at Shenavall being cleared and Strath na Sealga rented to sheep farmers, resident families had practised an annual pattern of use of An Teallach's hill pastures for many centuries.

The cycle began in April when high grazing began to grow. It was protected by a boy or girl acting as sentinel, warding off wild and stray animals to prevent them eating the new grass that was to be saved for livestock arriving in a few weeks' time. As spring turned to summer, community life, which had centred around the clustered houses of the clachan, began to spread outwards as herds were moved in stages up the slopes.

Communal hill grazing was separated from low-lying land for cultivation by a wall – the head dyke – made of turf. This was breached each year in early May to drive out animals that had wintered within the township, and was repaired rapidly to prevent stock trying to return over the next few months when cereal crops were grown within the dyke. Close to the houses was the infield, raising oats and bere (a forerunner to modern barley); and beyond – still within the head dyke – was the outfield, less productive ground where animals could be penned.

Within both fields, land was divided into rigs (rectangular plots) and distributed between the township's families in such a way as to ensure equality of crop yields. Each family had twenty or so rigs, dotted across the infield and outfield, which they cultivated manually or ploughed with oxen and horses. In some parts of the Highlands this practice, known as runrig, survived into the twentieth century but not so around An Teallach.

Once the lower ground outwith the head dyke and close to the township had been grazed bare, a second move was made in the first few days of June to more distant pasture near to the shielings (summer dwellings). Not only cattle, sheep and goats moved but whole families, making their summer homes in small round buildings with stone walls, roofed with branches and turf. Beside Loch na Sealga on the western side of An Teallach, ruined shielings can be seen as a circular jumble of stones that was once the low walls of a hut, with a patch of lush grass around it, fed by decades of cattle dung. The grassy areas have also been colonised by bracken whose shoots appear in late May and early June, adding to the bright greenness set amongst darker tones of bog myrtle and heather. Although their use was seasonal and temporary, these places have known the cycle of domestic human and animal life for decades.

Sequential use of early summer grazing ensured that livestock got as much good grass as possible, over as many months as possible, and relied upon detailed knowledge of upper slopes of mountains like An Teallach. The mix of animals gave access to even precarious patches of pasture, with goats being most agile and their descendants still renowned for adventurous grazing. Families lived in the shielings all summer, herded the animals, milked them and made butter and cheese. Girls and boys worked with the sheep, goats and cattle, moving them from one piece of upland grass to another and visiting remoter parts of the mountain used for stock needing less regular tending.

Today, both deer and goats forage for food on the highest of An Teallach's slopes as soon as vegetation is grown, seeking to

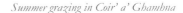

Summer grazing in Coir' a' Ghamhna

remain undisturbed and out of sight of most hillwalkers. By June, sheep and lambs are back on the mountain too, grazing in Gleann Chaorachain, Coir' a' Mhuilinn and Coire Mor an Teallaich and some on rock strewn areas below Bidein a' Ghlas Thuill, unconcerned by the passage of people. Occasionally in Strath na Sealga there are cattle, in a herd of fifty or more adults and calves within the area of the old head dyke at Shenavall.

The insect world is awakened by summer: bumble bees range widely, often flying above the summit and even out to sea; dragonflies hover in warm sunshine, with almost invisible flickering of two pairs of wings supporting a gleaming body of petrol blue, jade or grey. Much less welcome on calm summer days, much smaller and with numbers in millions, are midges. If the air is still and a human being is stationary, midges will locate and bite them within a few minutes, attracted by exhaled carbon dioxide. Wind and movement delay and deter their actions but An Teallach is as good (or bad) for midges as any other mountain in the northwest. There are also ticks, feeding

on animals' blood, putting a head through the skin and leaving their enlarged body sticking out from the surface for hours or even days. When the meal is complete, they drop on to vegetation in places where deer and goats like to rest, and they wait for the next warm-blooded creature to pass. A dog or human serves just as well as a deer or goat.

In spite of the risk from these tiny predators, for many British hillwalkers this is the time of year to reach An Teallach's tops without concerns about harsh weather. Summer has always been peak season for the mountain's human contact, and increasing numbers of people wanting to climb all the Munros ensure that Bidein a' Ghlas Thuill and Sgurr Fiona are visited frequently. On windless days the air may be full of midges, there may be mist draped across the mountain above its first few hundred metres, showers may sweep in from the southwest, but determined hillwalkers will make it to the two Munros. If the sky clears they will be rewarded with one of the best views in the northwest Highlands.

To north and west is the sea – Little Loch Broom, whose name comes from Loch a' Bhraoin, *loch of the showers*, and the Minch – stretching to the horizon and meeting the eastern coast of Lewis and Harris, eighty kilometres away. Turning landward, there are fields and houses by the shores of the loch and a vast and varied mountain landscape – north, east and south. An Teallach's northern neighbours are the monumental shapes of the mountains of Coigach and Inverpolly rising from the flatness of adjacent land and sea: the curtain wall of Ben Mor Coigach and the domed end of Suilven. To the north and northeast, there are glimpses of the hills of Sutherland as far away as Ben Hope and in the east, the Fannaichs, the Beinn Dearg hills and inland moors that stretch south from the River Oykel towards Seana Bhraigh, a remote Munro. To the south, rise tops and more tops of the Torridon, Applecross, Glen Carron and Kintail hills and close by, the mountains of Fisherfield and Letterewe, with Beinn Dearg Mor as a craggy foreground across the head of Loch na Sealga.

This is the quality of landscape that is treasured as the essence of highland Scotland by those who feel a deep affection for the character of the land, by people who have left their country and lived for many years abroad, and by city dwellers whose lives are equally distant. Moray McLaren, journalist and broadcaster of the mid twentieth century, put it this way:

"... the hunger for the beauty of wide moorland spaces, of mountains rich in the colours of the Western seaboard or grey and mysterious, of summer lochans dreaming unruffled in the high cleft of hills, peat-stained burns tumbling from one amber-coloured pool to another until they reach the river in the green glen."

Moray McLaren, journalist, nationalist
The Scots (1951)

Sheep on slopes below Bidein a' Ghlas Thuill

Corrag Bhuidhe and Sgurr Fiona: summer green

Sgurr Fiona from east of Bidein a' Ghlas Thuill

With traffic of vehicles on the lochside road and hillwalkers, Munro-baggers and mountaineers on the summit ridges, there is contrast to be found on An Teallach's west-facing slopes. The ground below Sgurr Fiona, Sgurr Creag an Eich and the northwest ridge that ends in Sgurr Ruadh offers human solitude as well as quiet grazing. It is the hidden side of the mountain, facing the inland glens, where the shore of Loch na Sealga forms An Teallach's western bound, cut by burns and scattered with small groups of ancient birches.

The area is shown on maps as Strathnasheallag Forest. In present times, 'Forest' signifies open hill land managed specifically for red deer, usually where there was once genuine forest with deer living in a mix of woodland and clearings. Strathnasheallag, *broad valley of hunting,* is mentioned in historical accounts – by early mapmakers and local writer Osgood Mackenzie of Inverewe, in the nineteenth century – and recommended as the best place for hunting deer in the district. Along with providing local people with venison, forests such as this acquired a fashionable image further south as Victorian sporting estates. They remain in use for annual stalking of stags from mid August to late October, and culling of hinds from late October to late February.

above: *Strathnashellag Forest*

facing page: *Toll an Lochain*

From the start of the sixteenth century to the middle of the nineteenth, these western slopes of An Teallach were part of a droving route from the Outer Hebrides to fairs and markets in central Scotland.

Drovers on the islands made deals to buy stock, travelled south with them and brought payment on their return. Cattle were landed out of open boats at Gruinard, seven kilometres to the northwest of Loch na Sealga, then travelled on the hoof southeastwards to Garve and Dingwall, moving about 16 kilometres (10 miles) each day.

The drove followed the line of the Gruinard River and Strath na Sealga, south alongside Loch an Nid and either east by Loch a' Bhraoin joining the Ullapool to Dingwall drove route, or further south by the west side of the Fannaichs to meet the drove route from Achnasheen and Garve. The animals went first to a Highland tryst (cattle sale) at Beauly or Muir of Ord, then by their hundreds to Falkirk. It was there that the biggest trysts were held each autumn as Scottish stock was sold to English dealers.

Together with summer grazings and permanent habitation in Strath na Sealga, the passing cattle droves were responsible for much greater activity on the west side of An Teallach in previous centuries than in recent times. The communication links established then have continued to be part of an historic network of rights of way, with important river crossings for travellers on foot between Kinlochewe, Braemore and Dundonnell.

These routes put present day feet on ground that has been walked for hundreds of years. There may be fewer people, lack of cultivation and less woodland but the skylines, rocks, wind and rain will be just as others saw and felt them in the past.

Below An Teallach's southwest slopes, the Abhainn Gleann na Muice meets the Abhainn Strath na Sealga, a fording place that has remained unchanged for hundreds of years

Up until the mid nineteenth century, tracks and drove routes were the major inland connections through this part of Scotland. Tracks were similar in condition and fabric to the paths that exist today, although narrower than those now used by motorised vehicles. In those times, travel through the glens to the west and south of An Teallach was always on foot or horseback as wheeled transport could not cope with the rough terrain. Horses and ponies were ridden, led as pack animals or pulled wooden sledges within farmed land to carry crops and wood.

Then in the 1840s, with repeated failure of the potato harvest through blight, events occurred that changed the old system of tracks for ever. Landowners in the northwest Highlands joined with government to make aid money available for building new roads, to give work and food to men and families who otherwise may have

starved. The road along the northeastern edge of An Teallach, continuing from Dundonnell by the Fain – named from the Gaelic word Feighan, *bog* – to Braemore, was one of these Destitution Roads and men came from as far away as Skye to work on it. The Dundonnell stretch joined others from further west (the head of Loch Torridon through by Loch Maree to Gairloch, Poolewe, Aultbea and Gruinard) to the road along the line of the Ullapool to Garve drove route. For the first time Loch Torridon was connected to Loch Broom by a well-made coastal route allowing carts, wagons and other wheeled horse-drawn vehicles to make the journey. Where links had existed by sea for many centuries, this was the beginning of the district being opened up on land with the possibility of easier travel and greater numbers of travellers. The arrival of the new roads, together with the gradual demise of droving, as sheep replaced cattle, diminished the use of Strath na Sealga as a through route.

At the time of the road building, more people lived and worked near An Teallach than ever before. From then on, as the resident population began to fall, the numbers of visitors increased: people with lives and work far away.

Summer tourists and hillwalkers come to An Teallach for many different reasons, each with personal meaning and context. More than anything, visitors want to take away pictures of An Teallach and its surroundings as reminders of their secular pilgrimage. There are plenty of viewpoints for photographs and even without these, human brains have huge capacity to store sensory information, particularly visual images,

and to keep them in their memories long after the visit.

"The magic of The Highlands, where light and distance lend an ethereal quality found in few places on Earth."

Raymond Eagle (1995)

Mountaineers can recall the profile of a ridge, the view from the summit, clouds drifting across crags and sunlight striking a glen below; tourists can bring to mind the lochs, sea, islands and the mountain's skyline. The importance of memories is proof that people come to An Teallach not only for the sake of the mountain but for themselves.

What part is played by senses other than visual, in visiting and remembering An Teallach?

The drove route southwest along Loch na Sealga, with Fannaich peaks in the far distance

Maria Coffey, author of *Where the mountain casts its shadow* (2003), works in the mountain environment and has explored the emotional side of mountaineering, including its tragedies. She has talked to many mountaineers about their motivation and every one of them said, at some point in the conversation, *'it makes me feel alive.'* Especially, they are speaking about their memory of emotions at the summit of their achievement, in those precious moments on the tops of high peaks, for which, sometimes, they are prepared to risk everything. They also speak of a feeling of transcendence, best described as *'a sense of intimacy with the infinite.'* This is not only for Himalayan mountaineers, nor is it just for those on the tops of mountains. It is akin to the pinnacle of feelings experienced when immersed in the sights and sounds of the natural world, which has been written about by artists, poets and environmentalists, among them John Muir, William Wordsworth, and William Blake.

"Nature as a poet ... becomes more and more visible the higher we go; for the mountains are fountains – beginning places, however related to sources beyond mortal ken."

John Muir (1911)

*"And I have felt
A presence that disturbs me with the joy
Of elevated thoughts, a sense sublime
Of something far more deeply interfused,
Whose dwelling is the light of setting suns,
And the round ocean, and the living air,
And the blue sky, and in the mind of man,
A motion and a spirit, that impels
All thinking things, all objects of all thought,
And rolls through all things."*

William Wordsworth
Lines composed a few miles above Tintern Abbey
(1798)

*"To see a world in a grain of sand
and a heaven in a wild flower,
hold infinity in the palm of your hand
and eternity in an hour."*

William Blake (1757-1827)
Auguries of Innocence

Being at the foot of An Teallach, or beside an old alder in Glean a' Chaorachain or on high slopes of the bowl of Glas Tholl, is just as significant as being on top of Sgurr Fiona. Part of feeling alive is having experience of all the senses – to taste as well as smell salt in the air at the shore of Little Loch Broom where the mountain rises from the sea; to hear as well as

Alder, Gleann Chaorachain

Alder bark and leaf

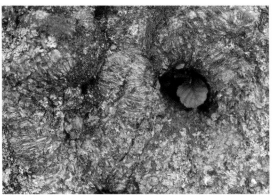

see the ancient tree creak and bend as a gust of wind buffets its branches; to feel with emotions as well as fingertips the steepness of rock and grass on the upper rim of the corrie just before reaching the ridge – and being able to remember each one.

Summer fades and greens in the landscape are tempered with hints of autumn. Heather is in bud and tips of bracken on the shieling sites are yellowing, just at the time when, years ago, families left for the townships. Most of the mountain becomes quieter – as birds that travelled to breed on An Teallach depart and visitors return to their distant homes – but red deer stags, carrying full heads of antlers and preparing to do battle for the hinds, raise their voices. Then the long days of mildness end and the weather transforms itself to a different intensity and energy.

Little Loch Broom below Meall Garbh

"The catalyst that converts any physical location – any environment if you will – into a place, is the process of experiencing deeply. A place is a piece of the whole environment that has been claimed by feelings."

Alan Gussow,
conservationist and landscape artist
A Sense of Place (1972)

5   AUTUMN

Heather by Allt Airdeasaidh   Bracken on Meall Garbh

Alpine bearberry, Coir' a' Mhuilinn   Rowan by Garbh Allt

Purple moor grass on   Deer grass, Coir' a' Mhuilinn
An Teallach's southeast slopes

facing page: An Teallach from the west (November)

overleaf: Gleann Chaorachain

AUTUMN

The season changes as chilly evenings and longer nights return. By September, the upland is streaked with new shades of copper and bronze in bracken and grasses, alongside purple flowering heather.

Seeing An Teallach from the west across Loch Ewe at the end of a period of high pressure, the mountain appears chiselled from naked rock, the water smooth and glassy. By seven in the evening the sea is opaque turquoise, set against deep mahogany of the shore and a taupe mountain. The familiar profile is centre stage, its peaks clearly defined: Stob Cadha Gobhlach, the spiked tops of Corrag Bhuidhe, Sgurr Fiona slightly behind Sgurr Creag an Eich, Bidein a' Ghlas Thuill, Glas Mheall Mor and further north, Sail Mhor with the long ridge ending at Sgurr Ruadh as foreground. The sky is totally clear of cloud and near the horizon, the colour of a yellow rose. Above, it becomes the same soft turquoise as the sea, merging through hints of green to a blue heaven. Over the next half an hour, minute by minute, tones shift as the light fades and the last traces of pinks and blues are extinguished into the subtleties of greys. By eight o'clock these too slip into darkness.

It is autumn: vibrant with colour, wet with rain. Gleann Chaorachain's rowans are aflame with berries between the pale yellow and ochre of its birches. In sheltered ravines, dog roses' delicate summer flowers have become bold fruits, spots of scarlet seen against rock and water.

This is not the same mellow season that the mountain's summer visitors will feel further south. Days of sunshine are followed by dull blankets of cloud bringing a flow of westerly driven rain and wind for the following weeks. October is a wet month and can also give the mountain its first snowfall of the winter.

Autumn has a rich mix of weather, air and light. Rainbows pierce the landscape for moments then are gone, coming as double half circles, flat bands of brightness and muted puffs of red and orange through to violet. Seen from the top of Coir' a' Mhuilinn, they appear in the north when showers drift across from the west. Moorland and crags on the far side of the Dundonnell River are illuminated with brilliant green and blue as the ground absorbs the ranges of colours that are closest to its own rusty brown. Minutes later, amongst swirls of dense grey, a soft globe of a full spectrum floats over the invisible faces of distant mountains.

" ... hills and water, sea and land, have been kaleidoscopically mixed with one another; ... the whole is overlaid by endlessly shifting patterns of light and shade as weather system follows weather system off the Atlantic: these are prominent among the elements which make our Highlands and Islands scenery so appealing."

James Hunter, historian
Last of the Free (1999)

Rowan, Gleann Chaorachain

Beinn Dearg Mor across An Teallach's southeast slopes

Underfoot, drenched ground and vegetation

leaf pouring a fountain from its tip which merges with others to stream across terraces of Torridonian sandstone. Straggling edges of cloud cling to the blackened walls of the corries and as they creep lower, the day darkens. When the sun appears, as it sometimes does, the ground is suddenly transformed, seared with gold, every droplet of water shining.

Throughout history, human beings have sought a spiritual dimension in life and it is no wonder that they found it amongst mountains. For those living close-by, the high hills have been homes of gods, where spirits were as much a part of the landscape as rocks and rain.

When Christianity arrived in this part of Scotland, memories of beliefs in sacred natural places entered the realms of superstition and folklore but did not disappear. Springs and rivers had spirits to be respected and rowan trees continued to be planted near to houses to help ward off misfortune, as they are at Shenavall to this day. Ancient festivals at Hallowe'en and Midwinter remained, brightening the months at the end of the year, and Gaelic writings of Christian monks recorded stories from the past, full of imagery, heroism and great deeds, with reverence for mountains and appreciation of nature.

'The glory of the great hills is unspoiled'

translation of a Gaelic poem
from 1,000 years ago

The line of the well-used path from Gleann Chaorachain, which crosses the moor before descending to Strath na Sealga, is face-on to southwesterlies, making the rough and heavy dampness of the air inescapable. An Teallach's bulk rises on the right hand side, felt rather than seen, with ridges lost in cloud and slopes of nearby rock wet and dark. As the far horizon is brought nearer and nearer, views of Beinn a' Chlaidheimh and Beinn Dearg Mor disappear, and the shift in perspective emphasises details close at hand. In November there are days when the whole mountain seems to run with water, and minature flowing worlds are everywhere: torrents from heather roots; cascades from ledges; every stalk or

Columba brought Christianity to Scotland from Ireland and founded the abbey on Iona in 570. At around the same time, a younger Celtic monk, Donan, created a religious community on the island of Eigg where he and many of his followers were massacred in 617, most probably by pagan Picts. In the years that followed, Donan's religious community re-established itself and sites further afield were dedicated to

Kildonan, Little Loch Broom

his memory. Kildonan, on the northern shore of Little Loch Broom, facing south with its view filled by An Teallach and once home to a dozen or more families, is one such place. Now deserted, its graveyard and houses are marked only by stones amongst the grass.

The Celtic monks spoke both Gaelic and Latin and their contacts were Europe-wide: west to Ireland, south to Canterbury and Rome. Their religious devotion touched the lives of local people and their languages brought scholarship and access to the written word to communities (mostly illiterate) where they lived. Some monks sought wilderness retreats to be alone with God, locations for prayer and meditation, with few distractions for the mind. Their traditions were coastal and they chose small islands like those in the Minch seen from An Teallach's northern ridges – the Summer Isles and Shiant Isles – rather than rock sanctuaries high in the mountains.

In the twenty-first century, in autumn, when few people are on An Teallach's slopes, there are opportunities to walk alone and infinite scope for finding quietness: time for self, time for a personal sense of the spiritual. Autumn weather is not always good for the high tops of the mountain, not good for long hours of daylight, but without the severe edge of winter, it is ideal for solitude.

"... to be quite alone where there are no other human beings is sharply exhilarating; it is as though some pressure has suddenly been lifted, allowing an intense awareness of one's surroundings, a sharpening of the senses ..."

Gavin Maxwell
Ring of Bright Water (1960)

Towards the end of the eighth century, the

Coir' a' Mhuilinn

Gaelic speaking Christian people of the northwest coast experienced much change. The land in which An Teallach lies was invaded and became a dominion of Norse kings and earls, with settlers moving in alongside established populations. Bilingualism was probably commonplace and in the mid ninth century, the names of Viking rulers Sigurd the Powerful and Thorstein the Red would have been familiar to those who lived amongst the mountains and along the shoreline.

Although Norse people converted to become Christian, their older gods were still alive to them through sagas. Odin was the wisest and most powerful Norse god, violent and mysterious, guarded by wolves and brought news by ravens, a god of battle yet able to fathom a person's soul and work magic. He hunted by night through mountains and woods, and would have been known to be at home in places like An Teallach. In contrast, Thor was the god of the common people and faithful protector of the peasants. He was strong, quick-tempered but quick to recover his good humour, the god of farming and fertility, with a chariot pulled by goats. Thor carried a mighty hammer and created thunder as his chariot raced through the clouds, so An Teallach had much to make him welcome too: its grazing for goats, autumn storms and an anvil on which to shape his hammer. It is easy to understand how, even amongst Christian teachings, generation upon generation of stories could continue to attach a spiritual or symbolic significance to the cry of a raven, a wolf howl at night or the sound of thunder rattling round Toll an Lochain and Glas Tholl.

An Teallach lies within the Medieval Christian parish of Loch Broom, by area the third largest in Scotland, a huge tract of mountainous land edged by sea in the west. It is bounded by the Little Gruinard River and the Fionn Loch in the southwest, then the line of summits of Mullach Coire Mhic Fhearchair, A' Chailleach, Beinn Liath Mhor Fannaich and Beinn Dearg in the southeast and east. Its northern limit includes Inverlael and Rhidorroch Forests before curving northwestwards to embrace Coigach. The parish church at Clachan is about twelve kilometres east of An Teallach and like many historic churches and burial grounds in the northwest Highlands is located close to the shore for ease of travel by sea.

In the neighbouring parish of Gairloch, west of the mountain, are the graveyard and ruin of the Chapel of Sand at Udrigle on the edge of Gruinard Bay. Those who worshipped here below the small east-facing window saw the peaks of Bidein a' Ghlas Thuill and Sgurr Fiona filling the horizon, giving strength to their

belief in God as maker and protector of all. This is one of the oldest Christian sites on the west coast, once thought to have been established by Columba but most likely by Donan. The ruined church is probably medieval, replacing an earlier building, and its more recent records include restoration and rethatching in 1713, funded by George Mackenzie of Gruinard.

For the people whose homes were in sight of An Teallach, patterns of life changed little from the eighth century to the eighteenth, with an annual round of farming and fishing alongside the Christian calendar and its festivals. Autumn was the season for returning to lower ground, taking cattle, sheep and goats by stages as the weather worsened on the mountain. It was a time when the quality of harvest, particularly cereals, was significant.

As the year winds down, the western slopes of An Teallach show little evidence of past boundaries between hill and township. Old dykes are mounds of moss, stone and grass, no longer capable of keeping animals close to the houses at Shenavall and Achneigie. The landscape flows from one texture to another yet its human history is neither as pleasing nor as subtle as the transitions of colour over rock

East window,
Chapel of Sand at Udrigle

"I will lift up mine eyes unto the hills, from whence cometh my help.
My help cometh from the Lord, which made heaven and earth.
The sun shall not smite thee by day, nor the moon by night.
The Lord shall preserve thee from all evil: he shall preserve thy soul."

Psalm 121
King James Bible (1611)

Graveyard and Chapel of Sand at Udrigle on Gruinard Bay with An Teallach beyond

and vegetation. Issues of ownership, politics and rights have woven their way through An Teallach's last few hundred years.

The mountain lies within an historic area, the Lands of Loch Broom, comprising the whole of the southern part of the medieval parish of Loch Broom and much of its neighbour, Gairloch. By the fifteenth century the Lands were part of territory held by the Earls of Ross and were inherited by Alexander, Lord of the Isles. For one hundred and fifty years, the Lordship of the Isles, with An Teallach at its northern edge, had given relative independence to the western Highlands and had allowed Gaelic culture to flourish. When Alexander acquired the Lands, his power was waning and there was much tension between the Scottish crown and the survival of Highland independence. Alexander's son, John, forfeited the Lands to the crown in order to keep his title

to the Lordship.

It was thus, in the mid fifteenth century, that the Lands of Loch Broom passed to the Mackenzies of Kintail. They were chiefs of the Clan Mackenzie, and An Teallach, along with most of the Loch Broom Lands, was to remain in Mackenzie hands for more than three hundred years, building a long and strong association between clan and mountain.

The clan system tied chiefs to their people by loyalty, family and territory, in relationships that were much deeper than simply paying rent. After unsuccessful efforts to re-assert Scottish independence in 1715 and 1745, clan chiefs lost most of their power, curtailed by the united crowns of Scotland and England, banned from gathering men to carry arms and forbidden to wear tartan. Some clan chiefs were removed and their lands bestowed upon others; some sold out to a new generation of landlords from further south; others remained, taking opportunities to profit from the introduction of extensive sheep farming but with few incentives towards keeping large numbers of tenants.

The 1745 defeat at Culloden was a watershed for ordinary folk in the Highlands too, as they became economic pawns in a land tenure system where heredity and kinship no longer carried any weight. In most cases ground was let to the person who could pay the highest price for a tenancy, and with the market for wool being good, sheep farmers from the south were able to outbid local farmers whose agriculture was based predominantly on cattle and cereals.

One branch of the Mackenzies remained in Dundonnell, still with many families on their land. They had stayed at home in the west during both the '15 and the '45 although they may have sent money to support other Mackenzies committed to the Jacobite cause and with whom they had family and business ties. In 1767, Kenneth Mackenzie built Dundonnell House in Strath Beag below the eastern slopes of An Teallach of which he was the owner. As a businessman, Kenneth was involved in extensive cattle farming and herring fisheries but equally important, he was well thought of locally, working hard for the neighbourhood and petitioning for better roads.

For other Mackenzie landowners these were years of evicting tenants from their estates. This meant that whole townships – like the one at Shenavall which James Hogg the Border poet, travelling through Strath na Sealga in 1804, saw recently deserted – were extinguished for ever. Cattle, goats, families, horses, oats and barley, furniture, tools, household goods were all abandoned or removed and houses and byres burned. Connection between these people and the ground to which they felt they belonged was severed and the state gave them no rights or support to fight for it. Not only were there tangible losses to bear but the loss of a sense of home and community; a harsh uprooting in a society where most people did not travel far.

The Mackenzies of Gruinard sold their estate in 1799 after mounting debts. Their inland glens, including Strath na Sealga with its string of townships, were ideal for sheep but had to be cleared of previous uses. Families were moved north to sites by the sea, known today as First

Dundonnell House in Strath Beag

Coast and Second Coast.

At Dundonnell House, Kenneth Mackenzie was succeeded in 1789 by his son George, a man of modest taste with no wish to turn the estate over to sheep. Countering the trends around him, George kept a large number of tenants and by continuing to live and work from Dundonnell when all other landlords in the parish of Loch Broom were absentees, he made his mark in history.

While George Mackenzie was at Dundonnell, there is just a chance that summer community life on the higher slopes of An Teallach may have continued. Elsewhere, with the coming of the sheep farmers, the use of shielings had ended and in the early years of the nineteenth century domestic cattle, goats and families will have come down together from the mountains in autumn for the last time.

George was succeeded in turn by his son, another Kenneth Mackenzie, but with less financial skill and consequent deterioration in the estate. Following Kenneth's death, there was much local ill-feeling as it became known that he had settled the Dundonnell property on his brother-in-law from the south, rather than a fellow Mackenzie, his brother Thomas. Resentment was vented on the new owner by killing horses, maiming cattle, torching buildings and firing shots at Dundonnell House, in what became known as the Dundonnell Atrocities of 1826-28. The strength of feeling was a measure of the loyalty of local people towards the Mackenzies, built up over decades. Court cases followed, with the eventual outcome that the estate was declared to be rightfully inherited by Thomas Mackenzie. However, financial difficulties persisted and debts were not cleared until the estate was sold – for £22,000 – fortunately to another Mackenzie, from Ardross.

As the nineteenth century progressed, more and more people departed from the Highlands, yet in spite of this the population peaked in 1841. Common diseases like measles, smallpox and whooping cough had been brought under control and infant mortality declined; but the birth rate remained high, so the same land was required to feed increasing numbers of people. Life was hard and food shortages almost permanent. Those who had been cleared from township tenancies were given small plots of ground – crofts – where they had to build the soil from scratch, while good quality arable land of past centuries was unworked, let as part of extensive grazing for sheep or left to naturalise as deer forest. Crofts were never meant to enable self-sufficiency but rather to provide a limited basis for living and the need to find other forms of work, usually tied to the landowner. Dispirited, many people chose to leave, especially when they heard about land being available in Canada. Ties of kinship and absence of ties to their new homes where they felt unwelcome prompted whole communities to depart together.

The potato played a fundamental part within these social upheavals. As a mainstay of diet, it was relied upon universally by the poorest families and enabled more mouths to be fed from a small piece of ground than any other food crop. When the potato harvest failed in 1846, the impact was devastating and the Highlands were gripped by famine for the following year. Relief came in the form of oatmeal from the south and through landowners and government providing employment in road building: labour gleaned from the starving to enable them to buy food. Harvests failed again in subsequent years giving no respite to people already weakened by malnutrition.

Shenavall at the foot of Sail Liath, An Teallach's southern top, where the community was evicted over two hundred years ago

Landowners were becoming increasingly intolerant of the presence of a debilitated local population from which they saw little economic benefit. It was in 1846 that three hundred people are said to have left or been evicted from the coastal communities of Gruinard, where their families may only have been for one or two generations since being moved from the glens in the shadow of An Teallach. Of crofters who were permitted to stay, some suffered a further move when their homes were cleared for Victorian shooting lodges, as at Drumchork, west of Gruinard in 1881.

As the nineteenth century progressed, poverty and illness prevalent in the Highlands became known more widely. Highlanders living further south began to speak out against landlords, clearances for deer forests and ruthless economic oppression of already poor people. Ripples of resistance against further exploitation also began to grow across the Highlands, with rent strikes and outbreaks of violence. Around An Teallach, perhaps because of the attitude of the Mackenzies in Dundonell, protest was not as strident as elsewhere.

Following much campaigning, finding strength within weakened and destitute communities as well as from others on their behalf, the government announced its intention to set up a Royal Commission *'to inquire into the conditions of the crofters and cottars in the Highlands and Islands of Scotland.'* On 1st May 1883 it began

Crofting land at Camusnagaul on An Teallach's lower slopes beside Little Loch Broom

work, touring the north and west, hearing testimony in public and keeping written accounts of every statement made.

Beneath the immediate suffering of thousands of ordinary people, there lay a class-ridden battle for land and rights, rooted in inequality. The mass of the population had become confined to the poorest land and required to pay rent equal to or above its productive capacity. If crofters improved their land they were charged more for it and could be moved on at will, having no right in tenure nor any right to vote (until 1885). They were tied, almost as slaves, to their lot; and maltreated, through attrition, almost to the point of genocide.

In many places landowners simply did not want the people any more and made efforts to remove them in large numbers to Canada, America and Australia. On the Hebrides in particular, landlords saw eviction and emigration as the best solution to the 'problem' of the native people of the islands, their tenants.

The Crofters Holdings Act was passed in 1886 restricting rent rises and giving security in perpetuity to thousands of families on their small plots of land. It was much less than the crofters, by now more politically aware, had wanted. They had never had rights like these before, but knew that they still did not have possession of the well-worked ground that their ancestors had lived upon and called home. It was only a partial victory. With the 1886 Act, the crofting landscape of the Highlands became a fixture and in nearly every case it was fixed into those austere locations to which people had been moved most recently. It was a poor substitute for the more fertile communal land worked in previous centuries but each crofting community retained the title of township and had access to common grazing.

The view northwest from An Teallach's tops is chequered by crofts which have now been worked for over a hundred years. Some are grazed by cattle, some are only in minimal use, none provide a complete living; but their tradition – of a lifestyle on a few acres of land, with the ability to keep sheep, cows, pigs or ponies – is the manifestation of a deeply valued right. It is a right to be here, and a right of belonging. The communities that have succeeded those which fought for their tenure are now growing, and the decline in population of the Highlands, prevalent for so much of the twentieth century, has ceased.

An Teallach's land has never been rich in productivity, except perhaps when a small population with plenty of labour was able to work the best ground, manage the upland grazing and sustainably harvest the resources of the woods; or at the height of wool prices in the nineteenth century when sheep dominated the mountain's slopes. By its terrain, location and climate, An Teallach does not repay human endeavour in supplying food with the flowing generosity found elsewhere on the planet. It is for less measurable and less material qualities that An Teallach is valued, amongst them, food for the spirit.

"... whatever we put into the mountains they give us back many fold."

Geoff Cohen
Northern Highlands (1993)

Birches in the ravine of Allt Airdeasaidh at An Teallach's northern edge

6 PLACE

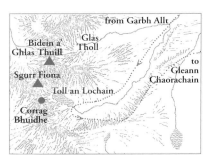

Scots pine and rhododendrons beside Garbh Allt

Waterfall near meeting of Allt a' Ghlas Thuill and Allt Coir' a' Ghiubhsachain

Pine relic, Coir' a' Ghiubhsachain

Torridonian sandstone, Coir' a' Ghiubhsachain

Cadha Gobhlach from Toll an Lochain

Route described in Chapter 6 (whole mountain sketch map, page 21)

facing page: *An Teallach from the west (April)*

overleaf: *Toll an Lochain*

PLACE

On a Friday in mid January, walking towards Loch Toll an Lochain, there was no one else in sight and it was a perfect winter day, cool with hardly any wind. Snow lay above three hundred metres. Ravens, deer and a few sheep were the most visible fellow creatures in Coir' a' Ghiubhsachain, *corrie of the fir forest*. A stag watched from a distance then turned away, leaving at an unalarmed trot, winter coat merging with the land, a steady ripple disappearing into the hillside. Tracks in Toll an Lochain advertised the recent presence of a hare, a fox and ptarmigan.

The only sounds were of running water heard from corners and folds of the landscape; then a raven overhead croaked, breaking the liquid soundtrack. It happened again when snow was underfoot, each step crunching loudly through hardened blankets on top of heather. Where snow lay on rock, movement was quieter, boots compressing just the top few millimetres of packed granules. Climbing higher, puddles were frozen into elegant patterns of fronds and lattices, and at Loch Toll an Lochain there was an icy crust at the water's edge washed by tiny waves of slate blue.

A month later in the same year, there had been heavier snowfalls. We sat on the steep south-facing slopes of Glas Mheall Liath looking over the upper ground of Coir' a' Ghiubhsachain, tired from working our way up through thigh deep drifts. The sun was warm and we had decided to go no further. The corrie below was gleaming white and full of smooth curves hiding all traces of the trunks and roots of previous centuries' Scots pines.

Below us something moved: a fox walking across snow on the far side of the burn. We caught sight of it between boulders as it began to travel more rapidly, out-stretched in a run on the pale surface. A few metres ahead of the fox, something smaller was also moving, most probably a hare, and the two weaved their chase into the rocky cover at the foot of Sail Liath.

Here is a route for any and all seasons amongst An Teallach's grandest scenery. It climbs by gentle slopes to half the height of the mountain, going through Coir' a' Ghiubhsachain to the shore of Loch Toll an Lochain at the foot of An Teallach's biggest rock faces and below the most dramatic parts of the main ridge. It then crosses the base of Sail Liath and follows an escarpment running parallel to the eastern prospect of the mountain, finally turning east-northeast along another line of crag backed by grassy slopes to come down through alder, rowan and birch in Gleann Chaorachain. The sculpted form of An Teallach, its corries and fringes of woodland are fundamental to the character of the mountain and the route threads a path amongst them. It is not so much a trip there and back again to Toll an Lochain but more an exploration of An Teallach as a place.

Near the bridge where the A832 crosses the Garbh Allt, it is wet underfoot for most of the year with bog myrtle growing to knee height beside dense thickets of rhododendron and Scots pine. On the north side of the burn there are several ways through the foliage and beyond the last of the trees a path leads upwards over slabs of Torridonian sandstone. The pines are tall and old with a lineage of thousands of years, whilst the rhododendrons – brought to Scotland from India and China in the nineteenth century to be used as ornamental planting – are almost as recent as recreational hillwalkers in the lifetime of the mountain.

After half an hour's walking the view opens up and skyline crags of An Teallach's two great eastern corries come into sight, 800 metres above the ends of three enormous spurs off the main ridge. The corries themselves are hidden by sharply rising ground: Glas Tholl beyond giant rolling steps of rock and grass and Toll an Lochain around the shoulder of Glas Mheall Liath.

There is a crossing place over the Allt a' Ghlas Thuill near to where it joins the Allt Coir' a' Ghiubhsachain, or if the volume of water is too great, a little further up hill. Gaining height gradually through the length of Coir' a' Ghiubhsachain, a path marked by occasional cairns leads from where the two burns meet all the way to Loch Toll an Lochain. It makes for easy walking, following ramps of sandstone strewn with glacier dumped boulders, curved and hollowed by centuries of erosion. Always alongside, rising on the right, is the massive form of An Teallach. The path stays north of the Allt Coir' a' Ghiubhsachain and eventually turns west towards the second corrie. Most maps fail to indicate its existence beyond the pool and waterfall at the meeting of the burns, yet for most of its length the path is distinct and shows signs of regular use. Cairns have been made from the plentiful supply of rounded stones and well placed for finding a way in mist.

Coir' a' Ghiubhsachain

For three kilometres the view is bounded to the southeast by the escarpment that edges Coir' a' Ghiubhsachain. The route's line of travel is southwestwards, enclosed by the long corrie glen and with the constant prospect of rockfaces below the smooth top of Sail Liath, *pale grey heel*. High to the west is the symmetrical cone of Glas Mheall Liath, end point of An Teallach's middle ridge, topped by stacked angular quartzite blocks making even gradients similar to those on Sail Liath, both recognised in form as well as colour by their Gaelic names. The escarpment is quartzite too, with the same hard grey-white surface as the peaks.

As the path rises to Toll an Lochain more of An Teallach's crags come into sight, not only ahead but at either side. This is the heart of the mountain, an arena of rock from top to toe, and once on higher ground, in the space of a few minutes, it is all around. Toll an Lochain is regarded by mountaineers as one of Scotland's most spectacular corries, yet, unassumingly, its Gaelic name means *hollow of the little loch*. It is the deepest space carved out of An Teallach's sides by the glaciers of ten thousand years ago and, more than any other feature, gives the mountain its distinctive might. It is an immense natural amphitheatre with the lochan as its centrepiece: flat and grey, or spangled with light, whipped by wind into furls of white, or perfectly still, filling the corrie floor as a mirror for its wild and beautiful setting.

In Coir' a' Ghiubhsachain:

distant crags, Sail Liath
below Glas Mheall Liath
Corrag Bhuidhe skyline

"There are only a few special mountains whose aura shines more brightly after close acquaintance. An Teallach is one of them."

Clarrie Pashley, photographer and
Martin Moran, mountaineer
The Magic of Wester Ross and Skye (2001)

On the far side of the water, layers of rock ledges and cracked jointed walls plunge in fierce inclines towards the depths of Loch Toll an Lochain; and above, the horizon is formed by the pinnacled ridge. To the northwest are precipitous slopes leading to Bidein a' Ghlas Thuill, An Teallach's summit, just out of view; at the west, the pyramid of Sgurr Fiona and the jagged line comprising Lord Berkeley's Seat, the tops of Corrag Bhuidhe and its buttress; then a sharp dip and in the southwest, Cadha Gobhlach buttresses, with gullies descending to the lochan; and finally, towards the south, the rock faces of Sail Liath.

Walking from the roadside to Toll an Lochain is a distance of about five kilometres and ascent of around 500 metres, all of which may take two or three hours; but numbers like these are a poor description of reaching An Teallach's most distinctive feature. The distance is the same as from the summit of Cairngorm to Ben Macdui and the height is double that of Arthur's Seat at Holyrood in Edinburgh. There is no fairness and little meaning in measuring these places by length and height, for *here* is what some have called the grandest corrie in Scotland and *there* are expanses of windtorn plateau, unique in Britain, and a landmark for a whole City. Each is its own place.

At the shore of the lochan are enormous boulders, good shelter from wind and rain where an hour can pass quickly, in driving snow, warm sun or tucked away from a gale. Even if the walk has been taken slowly, here is a chance to slow down again and give Toll an Lochain generous time for exploration. The dam where the burn leaves the lochan was built to ensure water supply for a turbine on the Garbh Allt, providing power for Dundonnell House. Juniper grows on the corrie floor, hard pressed to the ground, finding little shelter, whilst more

protected grassy ledges on the rising slopes of Sail Liath attract herds of goats. It is likely that no one else is nearby but tiny figures appear and disappear high above on the border between mountain and sky in the middle hours of the day. In the opposite direction, Toll an Lochain's lip ends like a stage, open to the distance, its audience the land mass of northern Scotland extending over moorland to the mountains of northwest Ross and Sutherland with the Destitution Road drawing a single human line through the landscape.

Around a century ago Henry David Thoreau wrote from another remote and wild place, in America: *'You cannot perceive beauty but with a serene mind'* (1906). Walking to Toll an Lochain is not a strenuous climb and perhaps its pace and process can bring serenity, to enable the corrie that characterises An Teallach to be seen in all its boldness of expression.

State of understanding, along with state of mind, affects perception. Throughout the twentieth century, from Thoreau and John Muir to Seton Gordon and Jim Crumley, opinions and appreciation of nature, mountains, wildness and landscape have grown.

"When we try to pick out anything by itself, we find it hitched to everything else in the universe. One fancies a heart like our own must be beating in every crystal and cell, and we feel like stopping to speak to the plants and animals as friendly fellow mountaineers."

John Muir, naturalist and conservationist (1911)

In those last hundred years has come greater knowledge of connectedness, intricacy of relationships and balance in the natural world. An Teallach, and all that mountaineers value

Facing page: *Sail Liath's northeast face, Toll an Lochain*

Toll an Lochain from Bidein a' Ghlas Thuill

about it, is within the scope of this complexity. John Muir's sense of joy has not been lost but added to, knowing now that every part of the mountain is subject to influence by human beings and every step taken is part of the impact of human action.

"The conflict is between the present and the future, between immediate and partial interests and the continuing interests of the entire human species. Ecology must aim not only at optimum use but also at optimum conservation of resources. These include enjoyment resources like scenery and solitude, beauty and interest as well as material resources like food or minerals; and against the interest of food-production we have to balance other interests, like human health, watershed protection, and recreation."

Julian Huxley, scientist (1962)

Understanding has also grown in recognising the subjectivity of individual perceptions,

moulded by awareness and life experiences. The more a person knows about the culture, geology, climate and social history of a landscape, the more they bring to their perspective. Appreciation of nature, here in the northwest Highlands, has layers of meaning: spacious stretches of blooming heather have come with loss of ancient woodland and quiet glens at the expense of lost communities.

"The way people feel about ... landscape, about our natural environment, depends very largely on the mental baggage that they haul around with them."

James Hunter, historian
On the Other Side of Sorrow (1995)

"To experience and understand the world around us, it is essential that we focus our minds. For only by listening deeply, with a quiet mind, can we ever fully experience nature."

Joseph Cornell
Listening to Nature (1987)

On a route such as this, mental preparation adds depth to the opportunity to spend time listening and looking. Within a day's walk to and from Toll an Lochain there can be pauses, and there does not have to be an urge to reach a particular point. Jim Crumley says that on his second visit to An Teallach he was convinced *'there was too much mountain to just climb it'* (1993). This route has no summit to mark achievement or create a single goal, and although Toll an Lochain may be the destination, once there, it is a big place.

"This leaf has jagged edges. This rock looks loose. From this place the snow is less visible, even though closer. These are things you should notice anyway. To live only for some future goal is shallow. It's the sides of the mountain which sustain life, not the top ..."

Robert Pirsig, philosopher
Zen and the Art of Motorcycle Maintenance (1974)

The more it is savoured, the more any experience becomes rooted in a person's mind. The longer the stay, the more Toll an Lochain can become a place in the memory of a hillwalker or mountaineer.

"Viewed simply as a life-support system, the earth is an environment. Viewed as a resource that sustains our humanity, the earth is a collection of places. We are homesick for places, we are reminded of places, it is the sounds and smells and sights of places which haunt us and against which we often measure our present."

Alan Gussow,
conservationist and landscape artist
A Sense of Place (1972)

Where the craggy incline of Sail Liath ends and the curve of the escarpment begins, there are gullies and small sandstone buttresses. A way can be found through them without losing

Quartzite steps below Sail Liath

much height to reach the sloping quartzite that provides a fine and measured descent. Within the next few minutes, looking west, an outstanding view unfolds of Toll an Lochain, face on, its whole form and setting in the mountain in one take. There is no better spot from which to capture the light and shade, the drifting cloud and whisps of vapour that cross An Teallach's famous corrie. From the distant east, Toll an Lochain is seen alongside Glas Tholl, twin features within the full expanse of their mountain range. Looking down from a few metres southwest of the summit of Bidein a' Ghlas Thuill, the corrie's rock walls are foreshortened and it is Loch Toll an Lochain that takes up most of the view. From here on the escarpment, all is well-proportioned, topped by the peaks and framed by enclosing ridges.

"What is 'best' in any architectural style will always be the most subjective of controversies, but it is arguable at least, from a podium on a cliff-edge of Coir' a' Ghiubhsachain, that in terms of the Scottish school of mountain architecture, here before you is its finest hour."

Jim Crumley, mountaineer
Among Mountains (1993)

Opposite the eastern slopes of Glas Mheall Liath the line of descent is broken and a smaller quartzite cliff leads down to woodland in Gleann Chaorachain, *glen of the place of mountain torrents,* to end the route. Where the cliff extends amongst the trees, there is a bridge over the burn whose features give the glen its name.

Here are solitary ancient alders with rowan growing from within their trunks, at the edge of denser woodland, mainly birch. On these lower slopes every step taken is where other human beings have passed, in the shade of

Facing page: *Toll an Lochain, from the escarpment*

ancestors of the present trees. Woods such as these have been on An Teallach's sides for hundreds of years, reaching much higher than now and busy with human activities: gathering firewood, collecting food, hunting or herding animals, felling trees for building and smelting. Over the bridge and up the slope is a well-used track running parallel to the burn, part of the long established right of way crossing the southeastern flank of An Teallach, linking communities in Dundonnell, Kinlochewe and Poolewe through the glens.

The track descends to the A832, reaching the road at Corrie Hallie, a few hundred metres south of the start of the route. The tops of An Teallach's corries are still visible almost to the end, framed by the trees. Seen together, they are a reminder of the mountain's variety in both structure and nature.

Descent alongside Coir' a' Ghiubhsachain

"Mountains should be climbed with as little effort as possible and without desire. The reality of your own nature should determine the speed. If you become restless, speed up. If you become winded, slow down. You climb the mountain in an equilibrium between restlessness and exhaustion. Then, when you're no longer thinking ahead, each footstep isn't just a means to an end but a unique event in itself."

Robert Pirsig
Zen and the Art of Motorcycle Maintenance (1974)

7 SUMMIT

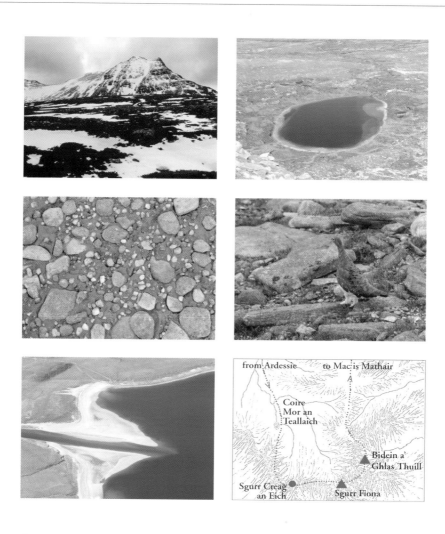

Sgurr Ruadh   Lochan Ruadh

Stones on An Teallach's   Ptarmigan on the upland plateau
upland plateau

Head of Loch na Sealga   Route described in Chapter 7
    (whole mountain sketch map, page 21)

facing page: An Teallach from the west (August)

overleaf: Sgurr Fiona above Coire Mor an Teallaich

SUMMIT

Coire Mor an Teallaich, *An Teallach's great corrie,* is stark and lonely, holding snow in grey and white banks late into spring. Its form is not an enfolding one like the deeper corries on An Teallach's eastern side and there is no sense of being sheltered in the heart of the mountain. It is open, catching the worst of winter gales, raw and bleak, with the north face of Sgurr Fiona an angular pyramid on its skyline beside the broad bulk of Bidein a' Ghlas Thuill. This is An Teallach's largest corrie, occupying the northwest quarter of the mountain but hidden from most viewpoints and only seen in its entirety from Sail Mhor.

"... taking a near course through a lateral valley, we found ourselves in the region of snow, on a brilliant frozen plain. The summit of the mountain, extending to five or six hundred perpendicular feet above this point ... is a rocky and narrow ridge, serrated into peaks, and of a very marked and picturesque character."

John MacCulloch, doctor, surveyor and
mountaineer describing (most probably)
Coire Mor an Teallaich
Highlands and Western Isles (1824)

The corrie drains into the Allt Airdeasaidh, *the fall stream,* which gathers into one torrent rain and snow from six square kilometres of hill. In spate it thunders over and through terraces, boulders and ravines making every scoop of rock into a foaming cauldron of yellow brown water. At the roadside where it passes beneath, now only a few hundred metres from the sea, coach parties stop to look in awe at the force of the cascade, so close.

This route follows the bounds of Coire Mor an Teallaich taking in the highest points of the

mountain – Bidein a' Ghlas Thuill and Sgurr Fiona, and also Sgurr Creag an Eich – and the ridges that join them, all at over 900 metres.

Bidein a' Ghlas Thuill (1,062 metres), *peak of the grey, green hollow,* is An Teallach's summit and along with Sgurr Fiona, a kilometre away and only two metres lower, a Munro. They attract many hillwalkers yet few arrive or leave by this route. 'Bidein' indicates a mountain peak that is seen above another feature, in this instance Glas Tholl on its eastern side, more widely visible than Coire Mor an Teallaich on the northwest. Sgurr Fiona, meaning *peak of wine* from 'fion', or *white peak* from 'fionn', has a much rockier outline, rising from steep surroundings. 'Sgurr' is a name rooted the west and northwest Highlands, with origins that may be both Gaelic and Nordic ('sker' means *rock* in Old Norse), descriptive of sharply pointed mountain peaks.

Together, the two Munros are the centre of An Teallach, the hub where its ridges meet and from which the structure of the mountain extends in all directions. At the end of a narrow rib of eroded sandstone curving west from Sgurr Fiona is Sgurr Creag an Eich (1,017 metres), the culmination of An Teallach's long northwest ridge and the first peak on the route. The sandstone crescent forms the rim of Coir' a' Ghamhna on whose side a prominent crag gives Sgurr Creag an Eich its name, *peak of the horse crag.* As vantage points, all three peaks are outstanding, with spectacular views of An Teallach itself and a panorama of mountains, glens and islands.

By contrast with the inclines of the high tops and their joining ridges, this route's ascent and descent are through a smoother landscape where the edges of Coire Mor an Teallaich roll towards the sea as rounded shoulders.

The route begins at Ardessie, on the foot of the most northerly slope of An Teallach, gaining height southwestwards beside the Allt Airdeasaidh. It follows a path that zigzags beside one waterfall after another to the glen between An Teallach and its sole outlier, the dome of Sail Mhor, *big heel*. As the glen levels out, the path vanishes and the land itself becomes the guide. The route from here to the crest of the northwest ridge, some three kilometres further on, is a gradual climb turning ever more southwards into the upland of Coire Mor an Teallaich. Vegetation is low lying and even heather is held prostrate by the frequency of wind, yet when the air is still this stoney expanse can feel secluded and quiet. For a few months of the year there is pasture in Coire Mor an Teallaich and sheep are grazed here. In winter and spring when snow is lying, a few deer scratch to find what is left of last summer's grazing, but they do not come in large numbers for this is not a hospitable part of the mountain and food is scarce.

In front is Sgurr Ruadh, *red peak*, An Teallach's northwest point, with a scramble up its rocky profile as one choice of ascent. Another is to walk further into the corrie towards Lochan Ruadh, *little red loch*, an almost perfect oval with a band of golden sand on its shoreline, sitting like a filled saucer at the end of a short spur off the ridge. Slopes on either side of the spur give easy access to the ridgetop a few hundred metres from Sgurr Ruadh.

The route towards Sgurr Creag an Eich is southeasterly with the sea behind and An Teallach's peaks ahead. The ridge is wide and bare, coloured by the soft pink of Torridonian sandstone and with its western side falling to Loch na Sealga. Across the loch, Beinn Dearg Mor and Beinn Dearg Bheag echo the form of An Teallach, shaped and scraped by glaciers, with corries facing east and ridges extending to the northwest, aligned with the loch.

The next few hours have the space and light of mountain scenery all around, some of the best that the British Isles have to offer. Being in places like this, even for just a day, makes mountaineers and hillwalkers set out from home, travel long distances, save up their holiday time, spend their earnings and work on their health and fitness. For some there is only one goal: to get to the top, a well-defined objective giving a clear destination to a journey in the mountains and satisfaction on achievement. Reaching a summit rewards effort with a sense of completion but prompts some of the underlying questions of this book. Is mountaineering simply about physical challenge and *just* about getting to the top? Can every mountain be expressed solely as a grid reference or GPS location, number of hours of travel and metres of ascent? The answers from these pages are 'no' to all of these, producing many more possibilities.

In the history of mountaineering others have raised similar questions, debating whether mountains should climbed at all or only admired from afar. John Ruskin was adamant that mountains were untouchable, to be viewed from a distance and as a whole, seen as a sequence of exquisite curves rooted in the eternal movements of the earth. Early members of the Alpine Club countered this with quests for first-hand and often dangerous experiences in the mountains, tackling hitherto unclimbed extremities of rock, ice and snow. They brought back knowledge of a mountain *as it was*, from their presence on its faces, ledges

Bidein a' Ghas Thuill from Coire Mor an Teallaich

and tops, as one by one they 'conquered' major peaks in the Alps. Theirs was a different kind of appreciation, built from absorbing the detail of reality, and known from physical effort and close contact.

"... every step of an ascent has a beauty of its own, which one is quietly absorbing even when one is not directly making it a subject of contemplation, and ... the view from the top is generally the crowning glory of the whole."

Leslie Stephen, mountaineer and past president of the Alpine Club (1894)

If mountains were only height and distance then climbing one would be much like climbing any other. But no two mountains are identical, either in form, location or environment, and even the same mountain is different each time a person goes there. Around 500 BC, a Greek philosopher, Heraclitus, interested in the fluidity and uncertainty of life, wrote: *'You can never step into the same river twice.'* His metaphor can be true for a mountaineer, as moving from one step to the next, either person, mountain or both will have changed. Change happens to the mountain and its environment – weather, light, season, erosion, plant and animal life – and change happens through experience, in the mind and body of the mountaineer.

Individual mountains attract and enchant. They are remembered and held in affection by those who know them well for their size, character, atmosphere, associations and history. Their less tangible, less visible and more emotional features are rarely expressed in the pages of hillwalking and mountaineering guides yet those who write of them make a lasting impression. The Cumbrian fells would be different without Wordsworth and Coleridge, the Sierras without John Muir and the Cairngorms without Jim Crumley. Reinhold Messner, Italian mountaineer famous for climbing all the earth's 8000 metre peaks and reaching the summit of Everest without oxygen, has said that *his* climbing gives meaning to a mountain.

There is now a well-trodden path to most popular summits, emphasising a single aspect of meaning. Mountaineering, once an adventure into the unknown, now carries a burden of being perceived as a monoculture of summit seekers. The top is a singular part of a mountain but equally unique is every place on

the way, with its own features and perspective. Redefined, mountaineering can be an experience of *being* in the mountains, not of *doing* them or their summits: an experience of depth, variety and choice of way of being. How many people on a mountain make only one choice? How many are aware of other choices they could make? To give meaning to a mountain, a person must begin by understanding their own meaning.

"The attainment of the summit is not the be-all or the end-all of mountaineering. It is simply a thread of gold in the day's designing."

F. S. Smythe, mountaineer and pacifist
The Spirit of the Hills (1935)

Looking back to Sgurr Creag an Eich and the northwest ridge from near Sgurr Fiona

Approaching Sgurr Fiona from Sgurr Creag an Eich

This route goes to the highest point of An Teallach but whilst the summit is one of the route's purposes, it is not the only one. The long ascent and circle of the northern part of the mountain is an exploration off the main tracks, on slopes rarely visited.

The ridge narrows to end at Sgurr Creag an Eich, An Teallach's western top, rising over Coir' a' Ghamhna, *corrie of the stirk*, the mountain's only southwest-facing corrie. A stirk is a young cow or bull between one and two years old and, although the gradients are extreme, here is rich summer grazing which may have been used for cattle in the past. Perhaps it was a solitary stirk whose wandering into this remote alpine setting gave it its name, or maybe there was regular use of the grass for younger animals that could cope with the nature of the terrain.

From Sgurr Creag an Eich, the route is a thin airy ridge making a curve to the foot of Sgurr Fiona. Ahead, on either side, are the arms of ridges that have drawn mountaineers to An Teallach for decades: to the left, Bidein a' Ghlas Thuill and the tops of buttresses leading east to Glas Meall Liath; to the right, An Teallach's rugged western faces, with more than 900 metres of parallel gullies dropping away towards Loch na Sealga from below a sequence of even rockier peaks. Although lower than the two Munros these have an equal if not greater pull on aspirations of mountaineers: Lord Berkeley's Seat and the four towers of Corrag Bhuidhe, *yellow forefinger*.

Far below, on the flat base of Strath na Sealga, two winding rivers join. Abhainn Gleann na Muice and Abhainn Loch an Nid drain the mountainous landscape to the south of An

An Teallach's ridges, with Sgurr Fiona (left) and Sgurr Creag an Eich

Teallach and their waters push out elongated sandspits beneath the surface at the head of Loch na Sealga.

The summit of Sgurr Fiona is small – a true sgurr, sharp and conical – and with a dozen people on a sunny afternoon, it begins to feel crowded; but the view is compelling, most of all, the end-on perspective of the pinnacles.

"Sgurr Fiona is An Teallach's finest top ... this amazing perch can have few rivals outside the Cuillin."

Richard Gilbert, mountaineer (2000)

From Sgurr Fiona towards Bidein a' Ghlas Thuill, a kilometre of ridge dips by 140 metres then rises again, with sandstone tors along its edge and glimpses of the water of Loch Toll an Lochain below. Under snow and ice and in autumn gales this is a serious mountaineering venture, along with the previous narrow stretch from Sgurr Creag an Eich, but in late spring and summer it is an exhilarating mountain walk. The weathered piles of Torridonian sandstone, touched by countless feet and hands as well as wind and frost, are the busiest rocks on the mountain, forming the main highway between the two Munros.

Hugh Munro had entered 'An Teallach Range' in his *Tables giving all the Scottish mountains exceeding 3,000 feet* when they were published in September 1891 as part of the first volume of the *Journal of the Scottish Mountaineering Club*, of which he was a founder member. Undoubtedly, Munro has given Scottish mountaineering a taste for summits, and mountaineers in Scotland a reason for collecting them. An answer to the question 'Why climb it?' famously asked of George Mallory in 1924 about Everest, is likely to get the response in Scotland of not only 'Because it's there' (Mallory's reply) but 'Because it's a Munro.' *'Bidein a' Ghlais Thuill'* at 3,483 feet, appeared in the 1891 *Tables* to represent An Teallach, as Munro's first list classified only one 'mountain' on each distinct massif of over 3,000 feet. It was not until 1981, with some changes in criteria in the third revision of the *Tables* by James Donaldson and Hamish Brown, that Sgurr Fiona became An Teallach's second Munro. The most recent edition of the *Tables* (1997) lists Bidein a' Ghlas Thuill (1,062 metres) and Sgurr Fiona (1,060 metres) as Munros 72 and 73, placing An Teallach amongst the highest ground in Scotland. From the Great Glen northwards, the hills of Glen Shiel, Glen Affric

and Strathfarrar hold Munros that are higher than An Teallach, but north of these there are only three mountains that exceed An Teallach's height: two peaks in the Fannaichs (Sgurr Mor, 1,110 metres and Sgurr nan Clach Geala, 1,093 metres), and nearby Beinn Dearg (1,084 metres). However, not one of these rises directly from the sea as An Teallach does, making every metre of its 1,062 visible and climbable.

"Of the height of Kea Cloch, I cannot speak with precision, having forgotten to bring up the barometer. But ... it must be among the highest mountains of the west coast, if not of Scotland; while it rises immediately from the sea by as steep an acclivity as is well possible, and without competitors, its apparent altitude is greater than that of any single mountain in Scotland, excepting perhaps Ben Nevis."

John MacCulloch (1824)

Bidein a' Ghlas Thuill from below Sgurr Fiona

An Teallach's northern tops, the Summer Isles and the Minch

Bidein a' Ghlas Thuill is the third vantage point of the route, with more mountain splendour all around. Across the space of Toll an Lochain, Sgurr Fiona and the turreted top of Corrag Bhuidhe sit above the corrie headwall, where hundreds of square metres of rock and crag disappear into their own shadows. From the summit to the pinnacles opposite is just over a kilometre and the view from eye level to the floors of both eastern corries is half that distance. The angles of sight are so different from the experience of walking on level ground that it is almost like flying.

A multitude of paths descends across the back of Bidein a' Ghlas Thuill and half a kilometre north from the summit, some 200 metres lower, there is a bealach. This wide neck of rock connects Bidein a' Ghlas Thuill to the entire northern part of the mountain. The route follows the upper edge of Coire Mor

an Teallaich around the side of a small top (unnamed on maps except as 919 metres) and north onto a broad ridge. Within a few paces the character of the mountain has changed from rough to smooth, and underfoot is an irregular pavement of sandstone, set in shallow terraces, giving a gentle downhill gradient. The ridge ahead is smoother still. The first three hundred metres are Sron a' Choire, *nose of the corrie,* a rounded platform above a rounded spur protruding into Coire Mor an Teallaich, alongside uniform slopes of Bidein a' Ghlas Thuill where runnels of pink grey scree push far into the grassy areas. If there is no wind or rain, sounds float up from below: noises of waterfalls and the bleat of sheep.

The onward view is filled by the water of the Minch with the Summer Isles spread across it and the undulating line of Lewis and Harris to the northwest. Dark shapes stand out in front of the distant long island. They are the Shiant Isles, whose name means *enchanted*. Their one-time owner Compton McKenzie described standing on the highest point and gazing in the direction of An Teallach, as *'swung between earth and heaven'* with the view being *'eastward to where the mountain line of Sutherland and Ross runs indigo-dark along the horizon like a jagged saw.'* (1928).

On the spacious high plateau that forms the northern mass of An Teallach, the mountain's immediate horizon is low and the sky huge. At ground level are thousands of small stones sorted by frost into mosaics of grey, rose pink and white, splashed with deeper pink in early summer as thrift and moss campion come into flower. A cairn marking an almost imperceptible rise on the ridgetop stands out like a broken statue on the featureless surface. There are no tracks to follow and in mist this is a disorientating place.

Keeping height at over 700 metres and heading north, there is scope to wander on the tops and spurs between Sron a' Choire and Mac is Mathair and look along the length of Little Loch Broom or across to Coigach. These tops are the antithesis of the sgurrs of earlier in the day, hardly distinguishable from their surrounding terrain, with no names. One is given a spot height on the Ordnance Survey 1:25,000 map and the others simply a loop of contour. Two small corries are tucked into the

western side of the high ground but only the northern one, Garbh Choire, *rough corrie*, is named on maps, as Garbh Choire Mor in its steep upper part and Garbh Choire Beag lower down. It seems that few people have frequented this part of the mountain and those who may have been here left no trace.

In late summer occasional flocks of golden plover and families of ptarmigan range over the gravelly ridges. The plovers rise at the approach of human beings and swirl into the air, landing a distance away. Ptarmigan merge with the surface and when they move, to potter discretely out of the way, it appears as if the land has trembled then settled again. It is hard to surprise them in these bare level places, so they have little need for a rattle of alarm calls and flight.

In comparison with the previous three kilometres, arrival at Mac is Mathair, *son and mother,* is well defined: a miniature peak perched on the shoulder of its parent with a profile seen from the whole of Little Loch Broom. Garbh Choire Beag now forms the foreground to the eastern aspect of Sail Mhor across the Allt Airdeasaidh. The route turns in that direction onto another characteristically stone-strewn ridge, descending to meet the burn just above its largest chasm, then joining the outward path beside the waterfalls to return to the roadside at Ardessie.

Ptarmigan on An Teallach's northern plateau

8   TIME

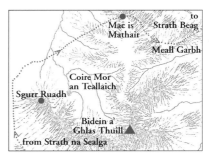

Shenavall door	*Sgurr Creag an Eich from Coire Mor an Teallaich*
Fireplace, Craigour	*Sandstone cobbles on old path on Meall Garbh*
Mac is Mathair, beyond the slopes of Sail Mhor	*Route described in Chapter 8 (whole mountain sketch map, page 21)*
facing page:	*An Teallach from the west (September)*
overleaf:	*Shenavall doorway*

TIME

From nearby Munros, Ruadh Stac Mor and Beinn a' Chlaidheimh, An Teallach is a large presence and its remote southwest faces fill the view to the north. Drovers camped with their cattle and dogs by Loch na Sealga and Loch an Nid will have known the mountain as a constant feature and watched shadows creep over the gullies as the sun sank in the evenings of late summer.

At the broadest part of Strath na Sealga and the southernmost corner of An Teallach is Shenavall, site of the township which appears on earliest maps of the area, its name derived from 'sean bhaile', *old town*. The present house is weatherproof and dry, tucked into the hillside and sheltered from northwesterly gales. Shenavall is probably one of the best known and best loved bothies in the Highlands, maintained by Inverness Mountaineering Club and the Mountain Bothies Association and owned by Gruinard Estate.

These days, residents at Shenavall are numerous, travelling from distant homes but staying only for a short time. In the main, they come for the mountains: An Teallach, plus six more Munros within walking distance beyond the two rivers that drain into Strath na Sealga.

Opening the door in the gloom of autumn brought a welcome stillness and sense of human contact into a day of heavy wind-born rain that had permeated into every fold of clothing. Hours of light were few and drapes of cloud had fallen over dun brown glens, hiding the summits. There was no one there; but the candles, chairs and house itself were a tangible memory of others' presence and it was tempting to stay. Half an hour later, with

inactivity emphasising every touch of damp and cold waterproofs, we reluctantly closed the door and set off beside the burn towards Dundonnell.

In May the previous year, with bare feet and rolled up trousers, boots lying by the wall and rucksacks open on the grass, we had sat outside on those same chairs, after a sunny day walking through the glens to the west. It had been dry and we crossed the Abhainn Strath na Sealga and the Abhainn Gleann na Muice near to where they meet, with water coming just to our knees. There are no bridges and in winter and early spring when melting snow adds to heavy rain, river levels rise rapidly and become chest deep, with force too strong to stand against. All can happen in less than twenty-four hours.

At Shenavall that night, rain hammered on the roof of the small room at the back of the house where we were sleeping. Next day the rivers were deeper and we did not plan to cross them, walking instead along the shore of Loch na Sealga and northwest by smaller hill lochs to the next house in that direction, Craigour, *goat rock*. Some ten kilometres from Shenavall and in recent times one of its nearest human neighbours, the farmstead (now in ruin) was inhabited until the nineteen thirties.

Time around a mountain gives a perspective that is different from time on it. There may be a good viewpoint at the summit but it will not be the mountain just climbed that fills the view, it will be others. It is impossible to see the whole mountain when standing on its top. Nor can a walk engaging in history do so by being on the highest peaks, for few people went there beyond a hundred years ago. To follow

In Gleann Chaorachain with a skyline of An Teallach's peaks

the experience of those who lived beside An Teallach in time gone by, feet must tread the base of the mountain.

This route loops around An Teallach. It makes links between the twenty-first century and those who have been here before, even as long ago as when hunter-gatherers lived in the woods and alongside the lochs. It is a journey in time and for many people it will be too long for one day's walk, being 28 kilometres (17.5 miles). Rapid travel is not part of this approach to An Teallach and an overnight stay in tent or bothy can allow for exploration, dawdling to savour the views and having an unhurried pace.

Starting from the roadside at Corrie Hallie, the route goes wide and to the east, crossing the lower slopes of the mountain before dropping into Strath na Sealga. It then comes close to the west side of An Teallach and, bending northeast, returns on the northern slopes by way of Mac is Mathair and finally down to Strath Beag over Meall Garbh to join the road not far from where it began.

On this route, choice is wide and meaning can be individual, more so than on a quest for a summit. The journey has a beginning and an end and it is the time between start and finish that matters, how it is defined and where it takes mind, body and spirit as they travel along the way. Company may be real and present, and may also draw on the past, in thought.

Leaving the A832 at the snow gates, about four kilometres from the Dundonnell Hotel, there is a rough vehicle track up to a gate. This and subsequent paths are an inheritance from shepherds, hunters, drovers and fellow travellers on foot or pony, used to access woods, grazing, mountain and glen. The track climbs, enclosed by Gleann Chaorachain, *glen of the place of mountain torrents,* with woodland on both sides and a rocky streambed below.

Beyond the trees, crests of An Teallach's ridges come ever increasingly into view. For many mountaineers these are the first memorable sights of their goals ahead, but for this route they are edges against the sky, part of a rolling perspective that will embrace the mountain. Gleann Chaorachain's woodland track is an historic introduction and the birches through which it passes are longstanding representatives of the vegetation on An Teallach through thousands of years.

The track emerges from the glen onto an expansive plateau of moorland and lochans, with peaks in Fisherfield and Letterewe to the south, the Fannaichs and Beinn Dearg to the east and An Teallach closeby at the west. Just beyond a large cairn marking the rise to the upland, the way divides giving a choice of route for the next couple of hours. To the right, small cairns mark the start of a path that traverses the lower slopes of Sail Liath, turning ever more westwards beside the Allt a' Chlaiginn down to Shenavall. Claigionn translates as *skull* and the rounded rocky hill on the south side of the burn near to the bothy carries the same name; but the word can also mean *best arable land of a farm,* possibly indicating former use of the lower ground into which the burn flows.

The alternative route continues south on the main track providing easy walking and fine

Birch leaves, Gleann Chaorachain

Strath na Sealga, its remnants of woodland and Achneigie (lower right)

views along the drove route towards Loch an Nid, *loch of the nest* (so called because of its position nestling amongst the hills). The track descends to the point where Strath na Sealga begins to narrow, four kilometres from Shenavall, then turns to face An Teallach and approach from the southeast. The mountain's western edge appears almost vertical, rising to Sgurr Creag an Eich, and its skyline continues to the quartzite tops, Sail Liath and Glas Mheall Liath. For a few hundred metres there is alder woodland, green in leaf long into autumn, bringing the full taste of a past landscape with shade of mature trees and the mountain as an occasionally glimpsed high horizon.

Ironically, the walk through woodland ends

before reaching the ruined byre and house at Achneigie, *field of the place of wood*. With the exception of two larches, two birches, some rowan by the burn and a few newly planted young trees, Achneigie's woods have all vanished. *Placenames of Ross and Cromarty* (1904) mentions that the house stood close to birch and alder woodland *'within living memory'* and there are references to trees in the names of nearby landmarks: on the hill behind is Torr-giubhais, *fir rock,* past which flows the Allt Doir' an t-Seasach, *burn of the fallow cattle's copse.*

By 1950, when W. H. Murray was welcomed by the Urquart family into their home and there were cattle still kept in the byre, Achneigie was the only inhabited house in the glen. Like so many other locations where lives and livelihood amongst these spectacular mountains have become unsustainable through economic and social pressures, Achneigie was later abandoned as a permanent home. The house became semi-derelict for several decades but has now been partially renovated as an estate lodge.

Shenavall is about half an hour's walk from Achneigie, the track following the eastern edge of Strath na Sealga. Deer graze on the flat land between the two rivers, moving slowly in small groups, often belying their total numbers: fifty, sixty, or more. Level riverside ground is what characterises a strath and there are only two uses of the name around An Teallach: here and at Dundonnell where the glacial trough filled by the sea extends inland as Strath Beag. All other valleys surrounding An Teallach, being narrower and steeper, are named as glens.

At Shenavall there are not only intact habitable buildings but also traces of the old dwellings of the clachan. These were houses made of stone, timber, turf, wattle and thatch, often shared with cattle and heated by a central fire of local peat or wood, helped by the warmth of the animals. Meals will have been of oats and

bere, milled into flour to make cakes and bread, with beef, milk and home-produced cheese, local fish, berries and nuts. Entertainment was in the Gaelic tradition of tales, song and music to which Norse people added their sagas. In this way, up until the sixteenth century, even small localities like the area around An Teallach were self-sufficient and much less reliant on imports than today's communities. The people of the clachan will have spun their own wool for garments and blankets, cured animal hides to make leather goods, smelted iron and made their own tools.

Present lives are more complex than those of the people who once lived at Shenavall. With a backpacking tent in Strath na Sealga or staying in the bothy, what holds appeal for mountaineers and hillwalkers is the simple rhythm of walk, talk, eat and sleep. The physical activity of a day in the mountains is a welcome change from others that are more mentally demanding or pressured; and in the evening – with no electricity, television or air conditioning – sitting out of doors on rock or turf, entertainment can again be songs and stories. In reality, a mountaineer's dependency on others – for food, fuel, clothing, equipment, transport, medicine, information – is intricate

Shenavall, looking northwest to Beinn Dearg Mor and Beinn Dearg Bheag

Old shieling grazing, Loch na Sealga

and far-reaching, and he or she would not be in the peaceful places on An Teallach without it; but whilst there, most prefer that linkage to be invisible.

A path from Shenavall goes northwest to Loch na Sealga and ends near the site of a boathouse. For the next few kilometres, there are no tracks and the route follows the western limit of An Teallach, bounded by the loch shore. There is quietness around the old shielings, the small patches of birch woodland and steep slopes of the mountain, but in this corner of the Highlands that has seen livelier times, silence is a lament of history. There is no intimation of the drovers, or the traffic on foot of nurses, teachers and tradesmen, or the voices of children born in the glen. There are no ways of knowing the day by day pleasure or hardship of lives lived here; and for many visitors, the

people of the past are both unknown in mind as well as invisible on the mountain's sides. James Hunter prompts his readers to learn about the meaning of quietness in landscapes across the Highlands. Prompting is necessary because studies of how human beings make sense of their surroundings in other locations, including cities, suggest that individuals take the evidence before their eyes and select what is consistent and relevant for their purpose. Thus, the present emptiness of the glens is more likely to be received as wildness by visitors who have come to An Teallach because of its mountain scenery than as depopulation or eviction.

"The unpopulated character of these landscapes ... every bit as symbolic of the eradication of human communities as they are suggestive of wild nature."

James Hunter, historian
On the Other Side of Sorrow (1995)

"Some of our trouble in comprehending ... comes from lack of enough visual reinforcements to underscore the functional order, and, worse still, from unnecessary visual contradictions."

Jane Jacobs, urbanist and activist
The Death and Life of Great American Cities
(1965)

An Teallach's western slopes are predominantly bare of the tree cover of their past. At the end of the sixteenth century, Timothy Pont's maps recorded extensive woodland in Strath na Sealga and placenames beside the loch (as at Achneigie) still include doire, *a copse or grove (primarily of oak)* – Doire Ghaineamhaich, *sandy copse,* and Doir' a' Mhadaidh, *copse of the fox or wolf* – recalling a different scene.

Below Sgurr Creag an Eich where trees have

survived through the long-term protection of rough terrain and addition of a high fence, developing woodland contrasts with adjacent areas that have suffered unrestricted felling and grazing. The future landscape around Allt a' Ghamhna will be evocative of the past and may give a stronger prompt to the mind of a visitor for whom slopes empty of trees do not yet speak of deforestation brought about by the activities of previous generations.

Responsibility in terms of thought as well as action has contributed to advances in the practice of environmentalism and preservation of wild places. For modern travellers in these mountains, there is much to absorb: not only something similar to the passion for nature's grandeur felt by Seton Gordon, or for the mountain itself as expressed by W. H. Murray,

Developing woodland, Allt a' Ghamhna

but more in terms of social understanding and more too in environmental awareness.

"We have never known what we were doing because we have never known what we were undoing. We cannot know what we are doing until we know what nature would be doing if we were doing nothing. And that is why we need small native wildernesses widely dispersed over the countryside as well as large ones in spectacular places."

Wendell Berry, poet and farmer
Preserving Wildness (1987)

"Most of us, however, still find it very difficult to accept that there is no escape – not even in so attractive a location as the Highlands – from the frequently pernicious consequences of our own collective conduct."

James Hunter
On the Other Side of Sorrow (1995)

Southwest of Sgurr Ruadh, *red peak,* the craggy end of An Teallach's northwest ridge, an old track leads towards Loch na Sealga. It has come from the coast at Gruinard ten kilometres away, past the deserted township of Glenarigolach, *glen of the forked shieling,* and the ruined farmstead at Craigour. The route joins it for a while, skirting Loch an Eich Dhuibh, *loch of the black horse,* and following the Allt Lon an Eich Dhuibh, *burn of the black horse marsh.* At the point where the track leaves the burn to drop to Loch Gaineamhaich, *sandy loch,* the route turns east, continuing beside the burn and climbing to a bealach between the lower slopes of Sgurr Ruadh and Ruigh Mheallan, *rounded arm.*

The lower part of Coire Mor an Teallaich is now in view and more comes into sight at every step, a barren landscape. The ground is

Below An Teallach's northwest ridge

112

Sgurr Fiona and Coire Mor an Teallaich

spread with pebbles and sandstone slabs above which a layer of peat has been eroded, leaving huge isolated blocks. On the skyline are Sgurr Fiona and Bidein a' Ghlas Thuill, An Teallach's highest points seen from an angle not well known to mountaineers, as this a rarely visited corner of the mountain and there are no paths.

The route crosses the open end of the corrie and takes a line northeastwards below two spurs before turning east through Garve Choire Beag, *rough small corrie*, and climbing to Mac is Mathair. From here looking north, the ten thousand year old glaciated landscape is a pattern of successive sealochs and mountains: Beinn Ghobhlach and Ben Mor Coigach, along with An Teallach, falling steeply to the coast. Settlements strung along the shores are the locations to which people evicted from clachans

like Shenavall were driven by landowners wanting to make greater profit from leases to sheep farmers.

The *Hector* sailed for Pictou, Nova Scotia, leaving Scotland from Greenock on 1st July 1773 with 179 people from Loch Broom parish on board. Many were from the north of the parish, around Ben Mor Coigach, their most common surnames being Fraser, Grant, McDonald, McKay, McKenzie, McLeod, Murray, Ross and Sutherland. Not all were forced emigrations.

An era of Highland life had come to an end and people displaced from the glens took their chance, having little to lose. Canada, with a passage on the *Hector* and others that followed her, offered a fresh start on good land.

"The people were not only cleared out of the glens, hunted and dragooned or shipped abroad like cattle, but those who remained, after being cowed into a mood of utter subjection, were by the most subtle and insidious means ... made to despise their language and tradition."

Neil Gunn, socialist, nationalist and novelist (1891-1973)

The hundred and fifty years from the mid-eighteenth century to the close of the nineteenth were harsh on the majority of native people around the mountains of Wester Ross. Poor nutrition, appalling living conditions, suppression of their language, eviction and famine gave people little strength and even less hope. The crofts alongside Little Loch Broom northwest of Mac is Mathair represent light at the end of a tunnel of hardship, and their rectangular arrangement of fences outlines the precious units of land that local people were granted as secure tenancies, through the 1886 Crofters Holdings Act. This remained the most significant piece of legislation for crofters until, after another century, the Land Reform Act was passed by the Scottish Parliament in 2003.

Today, the people of a crofting community can exercise a right to purchase the land on which they live, as and when it is put on the market for sale. The pioneering action of the Assynt Crofters Trust in buying the North Lochinver Estate in 1993 was an important step forward in the fight for land ownership for crofting communities and set the stage for the Land Reform Act a decade later. Along with North Lochinver, there is already a growing body of land in sight of An Teallach that is community-owned, including the peaks of Suilven, Cul Mor and Cul Beag.

The 2003 Act also gave legal recognition to a wider range of uses of the mountains, including for outdoor recreation. The Scottish Outdoor Access Code (2005) (campaigned for under the title of 'Right to Roam') specifies responsibilities between those who own land in mountainous areas, those who use it to earn a living and those who use the land for recreation. Walking round An Teallach's slopes is now a right (to be exercised responsibly) for all to enjoy.

Coastal croftland alongside Little Loch Broom from Mac is Mathair

Glas Mheall Mor from Meall Garbh

Mac is Mathair, *son and mother*, is a good place at which to reflect on the men, women and children who have lived and died around the mountain, and the global distances spanned by those who left or who now come to visit.

Although many communities, families and individuals boarded boats like the *Hector* bound for pastures new in Canada, many others stayed. Those remaining near An Teallach were loyal to the territory in which they had lived for generations, and over subsequent decades, family lines did not change markedly. Amongst the soldiers from Dundonnell district who lost their lives in the First World War, remembered on the memorial at the roadside below Mac is Mathair, the same surnames as those families'

who departed with the *Hector* make up over half the total: MacDonald, Mackenzie and Ross. By far the most common is Mackenzie and it is Mackenzies too that outnumber the MacLennans, MacGregors, Macraes, Macleods, and Macleans who are buried within view of An Teallach in the graveyards at Gruinard and the Chapel of Sand at Udrigle.

The next part of the route is again trackless, going southeast for one and a half kilometres over ground smoothed by wind, rain and frost. It drops a hundred metres off Mac is Mathair then curves without further loss of height to reach the broad ridge that bounds Coir' a' Mhuilinn, *corrie of the mills*. The northern face of Glas Mheall Mor towers ahead, rarely

Sandstone platforms, Meall Garbh

Little Loch Broom from Meall Garbh

The path ends at Dundonnell and the route turns inland along the road to complete its circle. At the start of the twentieth century Dundonnell was called Acha da Domhnaill, *field of two Donalds*, and a location near the farmhouse had the name Dun Domhnaill, *Donald's Fort*. 'Dun' usually indicates a fortified site of considerable age (often prehistoric) and there is undoubtedly a longstanding link here with the name Donald, but records show that the place was named Dundonnell by the Mackenzie owner around 1700.

The road retains much of its original line, sitting at the point where the mountain ends and the flatness of the strath begins. It turns inland towards the birchwoods where the route began, passing beneath stands of Scots pine, fellow survivors from the distant past, shading centuries of experience by others who have known An Teallach.

"For better or worse, wolf, bear, wild boar and beaver are long done from such places ... but birds still sing there as they sang six, seven, eight or nine thousand years back. The sun shines on occasion, as it has always done. And the sound of water in hill burns is unchanged. So listen to such age-old noises as you walk. Look out for the effect of sunlight on foliage. Note the subtly different scents of each species of tree. Imagine that the forest stretches on and on — almost, as it were, forever. And consider yourself following, as you definitely will be, in some hunter-gatherer's footsteps."

James Hunter
Last of the Free (1999)

reached by the sun, darkened with dampness or holding ice while the ridge opposite is bright and warm.

Turning northeast to Meall Garbh, *rough rounded hill*, amongst outcrops of sandstone, an old stalking path with gradients chosen to help human and pony traffic is the final descent of the route. As it weaves to and fro there are bird's-eye views of Little Loch Broom and the fields of Strath Beag, close-up encouters with collections of boulders perched on slabs — like a game of marbles left by a giant on a fairytale pavement — and underfoot, lichens on rock making jigsaw shapes in a palate of ochre, black, blue-grey and white.

facing page: *Scots pine, Strath Beag*

9 RIDGE

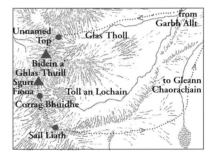

The Unnamed Top   *Geoff on Lord Berkeley's Seat*

Glas Mheall Liath from   *Lochan na Brathan*
Corrag Bhuidhe

Corrag Bhuidhe Buttress   *Route described in Chapter 9*
                                  (whole mountain sketch map, page 21)

facing page: *An Teallach from the west (August)*

overleaf: *Lord Berkeley's Seat*

RIDGE

The sky is pale blue and the sun has been up for several hours yet the droplets of dew on the five-pointed leaves of alpine lady's mantle are almost ice cold. Where shadows fall across the mountain there is a chill in the air; elsewhere, ground and vegetation are being warmed by the sun and complete lack of wind. A brown dog is belayed with a length of polypropylene rope to a substantial boulder, lest a hurried flight by ptarmigan proves too much for her instinct to seek out birds of the grouse family. She is a cocker spaniel of the working dog breed, at home amongst moors and mountains, alert in every muscle, eager to join in with what is going on. It is early June, just before seven in the morning, and an observant raven flying overhead might be watching two figures as well as the dog, the first climbing to the top of Lord Berkeley's Seat, the second sitting below the small summit of Sgurr Fiona, crouched over a camera, changing lenses, then edging downwards to an airy platform from which to lean out. There is no one else on An Teallach's skyline. One figure says, 'It really is exposed here.' The other responds, 'Hold on a moment. Can you sit down? That's good.'

Unlike routes to the top of rock towers on other mountains, the way up Lord Berkeley's Seat is a relatively simple scramble in dry conditions, not requiring ropes and climbing equipment as on the Inaccessible Pinnacle or Napes Needle, both of which might have been in the mind of the first speaker. Nonetheless, careful movement and a head for heights are important, as it is a clear 500 metres to the shelves of sandstone and water of Loch Toll an Lochain below. Lord Berkeley's Seat is set between the spiky cone of Sgurr Fiona and the four rugged tops of Corrag Bhuidhe, *yellow forefinger,* which together form the most striking section of An Teallach's twelve kilometres of ridges.

When mountaineers speak of the traverse of An Teallach, they usually mean the highest parts of the mountain from the trig' point on Bidein a' Ghlas Thuill to the southern top, Sail Liath. There are ten peaks in a distance of 3,000 metres, linked by a summit line that rises and falls in narrow steps and bands, with huge drops on either side. In winter the traverse is transformed into demanding mountaineering; in summer it is strenuous hillwalking, requiring willingness to use hands and feet, agility and balance.

Photographs done, we stayed for an hour or more taking turns at exploring Corrag Bhuidhe or sitting beside the dog, gazing at the expanse of northwest Scotland around us, waiting for the other's head to bob around the side of a rocky pile, look back and say hello. Sound travelled with ease in the clear still air and our conversation across the mountain was as if we were in the same room.

Kim on Sgurr Fiona

We had camped overnight in Coire Mor an Teallaich and climbed the steep grassy slopes to the bealach north of Sgurr Fiona before six a.m. Being up early and up high in the long days of summer follows in the footsteps of those who herded animals around An Teallach's grazing through the centuries. Perhaps they too were tempted on to the summit ridges, going higher than their animals or following the most adventurous of them, to reach the pinnacles.

The turrets of Corrag Bhuidhe, all at over 1,000 metres, are the centre of An Teallach's memorable jagged signature across the horizon of Wester Ross. They form a row from which the land has been swept away at both sides, and where foreground, beyond the next rounded sandstone block or two, vanishes over precipices. It is like being on the crest of a wave, lifted and frozen in space above the level plains of moorland and distant horizon of the sea. Over ten thousand years ago, below and around these turrets, ice dragged rocks away one by one from their neighbours. What remains was saved either by the tenacity of its connection to what lay beneath, by its height above the glaciers or by recession of the ice as temperatures began to rise.

An Teallach's central eastern ridge to Glas Mheall Liath

Ridges are one of An Teallach's specialities; not only the slim intensity of Corrag Bhuidhe, but broader mountain shoulders, with domes and peaks linked by continuous high ground. The mountain is laid out like an enormous version of Neptune's trident, pointing east, with a curved staff. The prongs are three ridges ending in Glas Mheall Mor, Glas Mheall Liath and Sail Liath and at their base are Bidein a' Ghlas Thuill and Sgurr Fiona, where the staff of the trident – the long northwest ridge bending in from Sgurr Ruadh and Sgurr Creag an Eich – joins them.

In 1891, Hugh Munro listed seven Tops on An Teallach (peaks over 3,000 feet not sufficiently distinct to have the status of separate mountains) as well as putting the summit '*An Teallach, Bidein a' Ghlais Thuill*' into his *Tables* to represent the entire massif. The Tops were Glas Mheall Mor, Sgurr Fiona, Sgurr Creag an Eich, Lord Berkeley's Seat, Corrag Bhuidhe, the top above Cadha Gobhlach and Glas Mheall Liath.

The names Bidein a' Ghlas Thuill, Sgurr Fiona and Glas Mheall Mor had appeared on the Ordnance Survey 1-inch map in its original edition in 1883. This showed contours every 250 feet and was a vital resource for early mountaineers, used by Munro and other Scottish Mountaineering Club members. By contrast, the O.S. 6-inch sheets, based on field survey work completed in 1877, did not show contours but provided many names including six of Munro's seven Tops on An Teallach. The remaining one, Lord Berkeley's Seat, was published by Munro even though he had not yet been there, and noted as a local name. The Seat has no Gaelic title and its relationship with Lord Berkeley – including who he was and whether he ever sat upon it – is a mystery.

Approach to Glas Tholl

It was not long before Munro came to An Teallach, enabling him to describe first-hand the individual peaks of the mountain. In 1893, a group of Scottish Mountaineering Club members including Munro explored the ridge, measuring heights using aneroid altimeters, taking photographs and recording times taken for each part. Their account of the traverse was published in the Club Journal with comments that Ordnance Survey maps were *'singularly incomplete'* and gave an impression of gentle slopes and uninteresting ridges. On the 6-inch sheet, most of the area south of Sgurr Fiona appeared to be blank, with no heights for several miles, almost as if the ground had not been surveyed. It is both possible and likely that it had been left uncharted by nineteenth century mapmakers due to difficulty with the terrain or unfavourable weather conditions.

This route follows in the path of Munro, going from north to south over eleven peaks. The ridge fills the view ahead and the route opens it up step by step, with each successive section able to be seen from the last. Ascent is through the corrie of Glas Tholl, gaining the ridge close to Glas Mheall Mor, *great grey green rounded hill*, and descent is by the grey-white slopes of Sail Liath, *pale grey heel*, to meet the track from Strath na Sealga to Dundonnell. This is a classic mountain scrambling route and a long day out, well known as one of the finest ridge traverses in Scotland.

"A thrilling scramble on one of the most spectacular of all Scottish mountains."

Ralph Storer
100 Best Routes on Scottish Mountains (1987)

Bidein a' Ghlas Thuill (right) and the southern skyline of Glas Tholl. Hayfork Gully is the long snowy Y between the buttresses

The route begins beside the Garbh Allt, *rough burn*, where it flows under the A832, then gains height through pines and rhododendrons, with an ever increasing view of An Teallach as the path rises on to open hillside. After days of rain, the deep pool near where the Allt Coir' a' Ghiubhsachain meets the Allt a' Ghlas Thuill is a mist of spray with its waterfall a loud tumbling spout. There is no need to cross as the ascent continues on the northern side of the Allt a' Ghlas Thuill to its source in Glas Tholl, *grey green hollow*. This is the northern of An Teallach's two great east-facing corries, with enclosing crags less seen than those of its neighbour.

On the southern side of the corrie are the buttresses whose tops punctuate the ridge between Bidein a' Ghlas Thuill and Glas Mheall Liath, *grey green, pale grey rounded hill*, turned towards the northeast and remaining cold long into spring, their cracks stacked with old snow. Hayfork Gully, where the first winter climb on An Teallach took place in March 1910, is the deep cleft rising to the second notch along the ridge, southeast from Bidein a' Ghlas Thuill. It was an outstanding choice for exploration yet risky, given the broken nature of An Teallach's crags, and the climbers found ice, but also loose rock and even looser vegetation.

Once in Glas Tholl, it becomes clear that there is an upper corrie at the back of the main bowl, under the shoulder of Glas Mheall Mor. Here, slopes are grassy with runs of scree and their southerly aspect offers deer and goats some of the highest grazing on the mountain. They also provide the route to the corrie rim just west of Glas Mheall Mor.

Heading south around the edge of the corrie, the ridge is several metres wide, spread with curved and rounded stones, dipping then rising to reach a small top. Although dwarfed by Bidein a' Ghlas Thuill and marked on maps only by its height, 919 metres, Munro included it in his description of the fourteen peaks in the An Teallach range and established the tradition of calling it the Unnamed Top. It is the first peak of the day, a gentle rise, from which the ridge then falls to a bealach with a fine view east across Glas Tholl to Beinn Dearg and the Fannaichs.

The ascent to Bidein a' Ghlas Thuill is steep yet easy. There are sandy terraces, loosened rocks, paths here and there; then, with no false summits, arrival at the highest point of An Teallach. The famous view of the famous ridge is straight ahead with the day's route swung around in a magnificent curve: Sgurr Fiona (1,060 metres), Lord Berkeley's Seat (1,030 metres), Corrag Bhuidhe's four tops (the highest at 1,047 metres), Corrag Bhuidhe Buttress (937 metres), Stob Cadha Ghobhlach (960 metres) and Sail Liath (954 metres).

The central prong of An Teallach's trident extends to the east from Bidein a' Ghlas Thuill. A short distance along, between the rock towers of Glas Tholl's buttresses, there is a view of Hayfork Gully with squarely cut, near vertical upper walls.

The route goes southwest off Bidein a' Ghlas Thuill and down by 140 metres amongst sculptured sandstone to the bealach between the

Glas Tholl

The Unnamed Top

Bealach between the Unnamed Top and Bidein a' Ghlas Thuill

two Munros. Loch Toll an Lochain is far below and the ever-narrowing edge leading to the spire of Sgurr Fiona is ahead.

"The weathered sandstone pinnacles which adorn the ridge looked for all the world like gigantic cottage loaves piled on top of one another."

W. W. King and H. T. Munro (*Scottish Mountaineering Club Journal, Vol. III*, 1893)

The account of the traverse of An Teallach in 1893 has two photographs accompanying it. The first, taken by W. Douglas, is of Loch Toll an Lochain with crags rising from water level to horizon, 520 metres above. It shows the ridge broadside on, from the bealach between Bidein a' Ghlas Thuill and Sgurr Fiona to the pair of gullies just south of Corrag Bhuidhe Buttress, and has the crest of Corrag Bhuidhe at centre top of the image. Douglas and Rennie, the two photographers, left early in the day to traverse the ridge in the opposite direction from Munro and the main party, so as to reach Toll an Lochain in the morning, in time to see it with full light on the lochan and crags.

The second photograph, by J. Rennie, is a view of the main ridge from not far below the summit of Bidein a' Ghlas Thuill, taken in the afternoon. The image is an elongated rectangle, similar in format to many modern landscape photographs, showing the ridge rising to the summit of Sgurr Fiona and the skyline of nine peaks, ending with Sail Liath. Both are fine black and white plates, with grooves and ledges on the faces of the mountain emphasised by large patches of snow. The date was 1st April and there was ice glazing the rocks as they approached the summit of Sgurr Fiona.

These two images have characterised An Teallach, and many others have joined Douglas and Rennie in taking similar photographs. They show the rockiest aspects of the mountain's architecture, immense areas of crag, the flow of peaks along the ridge and the same centrepiece, Corrag Bhuidhe. They appear in mountain guidebooks, calendars, as cards and prints, and in countless hundreds of personal photographic collections. The route continues along their skyline.

Somewhere near Sgurr Fiona most people begin to put hands as well as feet on to rock, becoming absorbed in the rhythm of movement over rises and falls of the ridge. The scenery is breathtaking, the situation dramatic and there is very little room for mistakes. In dry summer weather, the route across the tops of Lord Berkeley's Seat and the four Corrag Bhuidhe towers demands much care but is not technically difficult; however, in wet, windy or freezing conditions there is greater risk, and under full snow it is a substantial undertaking. Unfortunately, An Teallach is well known for having a history of fatal accidents. A small error, even from an experienced mountaineer, can end with tragedy, and as numbers of hillwalkers and mountaineers on An Teallach have increased, so too has the toll of lives lost.

Munro and his group came well-equipped with ropes and ice axes, not knowing what they would find. The day was wintry even though it was April. There was a cornice on the rim of Glas Tholl and frequent squalls carried blown snow into their faces. They were delighted.

Although it is no longer a journey of exploration as it was in 1893, An Teallach offers an exceptional challenge, being one of only half a dozen ridges in Scotland where the highest points are continuous pinnacled rock. What is special about them is the commitment, skill and effort required, which, like the pinnacles, are unavoidable in making a traverse of the tops.

Right to left, ascent to Sgurr Fiona with Lord Berkeley's Seat and Corrag Bhuidhe

In moving over difficult terrain in high mountain environments, sustained concentration of mind and co-ordination of movement combine, completely absorbing attention and bringing a sense of liberation from all else but the present moment. Perception is sharpened many-fold and there is acute awareness of every action. For some people, this state of being, enhanced by the surroundings of a rare and beautiful place, and especially after hours of effort, has a spiritual dimension. Mountaineers speak of being at one with the mountain and call it 'the flow.' The name was chosen by Croatian-born Mihaly Csikszentmihalyi, a leading research psychologist working in the United States in the fields of optimal experiences, happiness

and creativity. In 1990 he defined and described 'the flow' as a mental state characterised by feelings of great freedom, enjoyment, fulfilment and skill. He developed the theory that human beings are at their most happy when in a flow state, fully immersed with the activity in hand and the situation. This extraordinary focus of mind and body has qualities that are both meditative and addictive; once felt, it is sought again and again. For a capable mountaineer or hillwalker who delights in moving on rock, the route from Sgurr Fiona over Lord Berkeley's Seat and the pinnacles of Corrag Bhuidhe can create a flavour of 'the flow.' Munro's party in 1893 called it the finest part of their climb, *'a beautifully serrated ridge.'*

The ridge from Sgurr Fiona (right to left): Lord Berkeley's Seat and Corrag Bhuidhe, Stob Cadha Gobhlach, Sail Liath

"In climbing where the danger is great, all attention has to be given the ground step by step, leaving nothing for beauty by the way. But this care, so keenly and narrowly concentrated, is not without advantages. One is thoroughly aroused. Compared with the alertness of the senses and corresponding precision and power of the muscles on such occasions, one may be said to sleep all the rest of the year. The mind and body remain awake for some time after the dangerous ground is past, so that arriving on the summit with the grand outlook – all the world spread below – one is able to see it better, and brings to the feast a far keener vision, and reaps richer harvests than would have been possible ere the presence of danger summoned one to life."

John Muir (1834 -1914)

As mind, body and mountain work their magic, it is not the time to stop and analyse how this comes about, for to do so would break the spell. Simply let the senses roll.

Descent from the last peak of Corrag Bhuidhe is the trickiest part of the ridge, requiring a short climb over large blocks in a severely exposed situation. From here onwards, the crest is broader and the slopes that flank it a little less precipitous, particularly on the western side. Corrag Bhuidhe Buttress juts out into the space above Loch Toll an Lochain and is a wonderful spot from which to look back at the last hour's effort. It can be a place to relax too, for the remainder of the ridge – over the domes of Stob Cadha Gobhlach and Sail Liath – is not so strenuous, as well as being slightly less exposed.

In the account by Munro and King, Cadha Gobhlach – the high col before the final ascent to Sail Liath – is translated as the *difficult, forky, or narrow pass* and it is here that this route leaves theirs. Munro's party descended from the ridge at Cadha Gobhlach (having first made an ascent of Sail Liath) by a gully into Toll an Lochain 400 metres below, cutting steps in hard snow for 100 metres then making a long glissade. Their friends with the cameras had come up this way and told them that the snow cover was continuous to the corrie floor. They reached the shore of the lochan at 6.15 p.m., nearly nine hours after leaving Dundonnell, and wrote later: *'huge buttresses of rock encircle this lonely sheet of water and rise sheer from its west and south shores'* and *'a grand piece of rock scenery.'* As for so many people, Toll an Lochain left a strong impression with them.

Munro had published his *Tables* in 1891, two years before he visited An Teallach, and since that first edition, they have had four major revisions: 1921, 1974, 1981 and 1997. Both Munros and Tops are subject to the editorial judgement of those who have been responsible for each revision, and to much re-measurement. Munro died two years before the publication of the second edition of the *Tables* in which there were a large number of changes, many based on his own continuing work over nearly three decades. The 'Top above Cadha Gobhlach' from the 1891 *Tables* is renamed Stob Cadha Gobhlach, *peak of the forked pass*, in later editions. Sail Liath, which had been mentioned as slightly below 3,000 feet in the first *Tables*, was found to be 3,100 feet by Munro's aneroid barometer in 1893 and was introduced into the 1921 *Tables* as a Top even though its height was still approximate, measured only by climbers and not fully surveyed. Corrag Bhuidhe Buttress, which Munro had not included in his original list, appeared as a Top in the *Tables* of 1921, 1974 and 1981, but was deleted in 1997. By 1981 the O.S. 1:50,000 Landranger series of metric maps had become available and heights

'... this lonely sheet of water' – Toll an Lochain as it might have been seen by Munro's party in 1893

of all Munros and Tops in the edition of that year were given in metres. It was also the year that Sgurr Fiona (a Top in all previous editions) entered the *Tables* as An Teallach's second Munro.

The route continues from Cadha Gobhlach to the last peak, Sail Liath, then southeast for nearly a kilometre on evenly graded quartzite slopes, dazzlingly white in sunshine. The ground steepens again at the very end of the ridge and the route turns east, picking a way towards Lochan na Brathan, *little loch of the quern*, to join the track from Strath na Sealga that skirts the foot of the mountain.

Corrag Bhuidhe is now several kilometres away, yet still its profile dominates all views to the west. The track descends into Gleann Chaorachan, returning to the roadside a kilometre south of the bridge over the Garbh Allt where the route began.

" ... more important than mere Munros is the four kilometre ridge around the mountain's eastern corrie, a sinuous, sharp edge which offers the hillwalker an exhilarating day's outing, without doubt one of the best expeditions in the country."

Cameron McNeish,
broadcaster and mountaineer (1996)

facing page:
*Slopes below Cadha Gobhlach,
Munro's route of descent in 1893*

Descent from Sail Liath

10   CONNECTION

Ruined roadside building at Fain, with
An Teallach beyond

Goats on the slopes of Sail Liath

Byre wall, Shenavall

facing page:

overleaf:

Loch Toll an Lochain from Stob Cadha
Gobhlach

Corrag Bhuidhe and Sgurr Fiona from
Sail Liath

Route described in Chapter 10
(whole mountain sketch map, page 21)

An Teallach from the west (June)

Toll an Lochain from Fain

CONNECTION

Between the Fannaichs and the glen of the Abhainn Loch an Nid, framed by a line of three Munros – Mullach Coire Mhic Fhearchair, Sgurr Ban and Beinn a' Chlaidheimh – with An Teallach at the northwest, the bleak high moor has never had a resident community; it has been somewhere to pass through. The isolated ruined house at Fain was an inn, a rough and wild place, where travellers stayed when the journey had been long or the weather bad. The road has no shelter except intermittent fences to protect it from becoming impassable in wind-driven snow. For a few months in the mid nineteenth century road builders populated the empty land, working within daily sight of the broad bulk of An Teallach spread between themselves and the sea, as ever present as their hunger. From this side, the mountain has its foundations in the moor, its huge glacier torn corries gaping wide, its ridges recognisable from afar. The line of the road, as bold across the landscape of today as the ancient silhouette of the mountain, is a tangible connection with the past, with men who laboured for survival in desperately poor economic and social conditions.

Roads and paths engrain the history of human endeavour into the earth. On An Teallach it is the peaks and their main approaches that bear these markings, as metal has scratched rock – nails in boots from the early twentieth century, ice axes, crampons and points of trekking poles – and soles have crushed plant life and worn gravel and thin soil into pathways. In witness to its human traffic, the crest of An Teallach's ridge is drawn as clearly underfoot as by a graphic artist. The higher the altitude, the longer the marks last, because vegetation does not reappear rapidly on exposed upper slopes, and smoothing by weather is a slow process. A thousand metres lower, in surrounding glens where many more feet have passed – where people have lived, walked, worked, herded cattle and raised crops – evidence of their repeated pressure is gone in a few seasons. Plants come back with their flowers and seeds, except to those thoroughfares where feet continue to walk.

"Once trodden by human feet, a natural path becomes a work of man, each traveller marking the way for the next ... Feet follow footsteps, and so a road is trodden into history."

J. R. L. Anderson, writer
and Fay Godwin, photographer
The Oldest Road,
An Exploration of the Ridgeway (1975)

An explorer delights in finding a way where no one has gone before, or where signs and memories of previous passing have vanished. Now, in the mountains of Scotland and especially on the Munros, there is a path to almost every summit and exploring is no longer an option. A cover of snow, elusive amongst warmer winters, obliterates the wear created by others and invites feelings of pioneering and discovery. Navigation is sharpened and mountaineering conversations cease as attention to the present – to the slope, the angle of a burn, rocks as landmarks – takes precedence.

This route is in part ephemeral – a personal exploration – and in part a reinforcement of the strongest connections between the tread of human feet and An Teallach. It is capricious; there are no paths for some of its distance and it avoids the major peaks, leaves the ridge after less than a kilometre and chooses ascent and

An Teallach from across the moorland to the east

descent by rough ground. It follows the drove route then turns away to become undefined and distant from the mountain, yet keeps a strong focus on the nature of the terrain as it winds over trackless moorland.

Starting inland, facing the big corries, the route approaches the southeastern end of the ridge by ascending rock shelves that form the rim of Toll an Lochain, reaching the top of Sail Liath and following the ridge as far as the bealach between Stob Cadha Gobhlach and Corrag Bhuidhe Buttress. Here it descends on the sides of Coir' a' Ghamhna to the shore of Loch na Sealga and joins the old right of way for several kilometres on the flat land of the strath. Past

Shenavall and Achneigie, it bends to face the mountain and climbs up hill for a while, ending by curving east to wander the high moor, around quiet lochans and rocky terraces, with An Teallach as a massive backdrop.

The route begins beside the A832 at Fain Bridge over the Dundonnell River and goes west to the telecommunications mast (which is soon passed) then on to slopes of grass and heather. The prospect ahead is hidden until the last moment: the spacious upland bounded by mountains, An Teallach the largest, seen whole, with ridges broadside on, from Glas Mheall Mor at the north to Sail Liath at the south.

"Overtopping all the neighbouring land, it commands a wide extent of the interior country, ... and losing itself eastward in a series of deep valleys, ridges, and ravines of bare white rock, characterised by an aspect of desolation not easily exceeded ..."

John MacCulloch
doctor, surveyor and mountaineer
Highlands and Western Isles (1824)

"The summits stood clear and the sun shone and the wet wind was shaping the new snow ... and An Teallach's five mile horizon was the perfect mountain, and this was the perfect approach to it."

Jim Crumley, mountaineer
Among Mountains (1993)

There are more than fifty lochans scattered across the six or so square kilometres through which the route now passes. Every few hundred metres the land poses a question: which way to go? There is no path and no clarity of topography to create a simple answer; instead there are choices – a dry band of rock, a shallow place to ford a burn – making the route an individual one. The rises and falls are slight and rock outcrops minimalist, as the route travels west, gradually turning northwest, heading directly towards Toll an Lochain. Landmarks are important, however small or subtle, as are memories of them, for the route returns by the same ground.

Weaving between the lochans, the moving line of tread may be made only this once, leaving little more than a bootmark here and there, and not for any length of time. The almost invisible contact with the earth will be kept in mind – a

Turning northwest towards Toll an Lochain

137

virtual pathway – for a day, a week, a month or as long as its originator wants to remember.

"The mountain comes so highly recommended by all who have climbed here, but few who have climbed have then watched the mountain grow from the moor and learned how much there really is to recommend."

Jim Crumley
Among Mountains (1993)

As the route progresses over the moorland, it crosses two tracks linking Strath na Sealga with Strath Beag. The southern one, well-graded for ponies and occasional vehicles, will be joined for a while, later in the day. Coming nearer to the foot of Sail Liath, slopes steepen and where the gradient changes, the relationship between walker and mountain changes too, from making an approach at a distance apart, to standing on An Teallach's rising side.

Lochan na Brathan is a place to pause before moving towards the edge of the hill where the outer walls of Toll an Lochain begin. Seen from this southern brink of the corrie, Loch Toll an Lochain is a wide expanse of water and the ridge from Glas Mheall Liath to Bidein a' Ghlas Thuill is stretched to its full extent. The route keeps going upwards, picking a way, rock by rock, tussock by tussock, to gain the top of Sail Liath.

A hundred years ago when mountaineering began to develop, it was the pleasure of exploration that enticed people to climb, not always taking the most obvious or shortest ways to the top of a mountain. Albert Mummery (1855-1895), the British mountaineer who pioneered Alpine and Himalayan ascents using challenging and difficult routes and who is often considered to be the father of modern rock climbing, wrote:

Slopes of Sail Liath, looking back to Lochan na Brathan

An Teallach's main ridge from Sail Liath:
Stob Cadha Gobhlach (left), Corrag Buidhe buttress in sunlight, Corrag Bhuidhe, Sgurr Fiona and Sgurr Creag an Eich (far centre).

"... the true mountaineer is a wanderer ... who loves to be where no human being has been before, who delights in gripping rocks that have previously never felt the touch of human fingers."

A. F. Mummery, mountaineer
My Climbs in the Alps and Caucasus (1895)

Approaching Sail Liath by platforms and ledges where cornices form in hard winters, there are few traces of others' passage, but once at the top, the character of the route is different. In company with many, their footmarks now an intrinsic part of the mountain, and with no ambiguity of line, An Teallach's ridgetop path follows the rise and fall of the mountain for 800 metres, as does the route, to the bealach below Corrag Bhuidhe. The upper eastern faces are close and the profile of the ridge alters with each swing of direction, west to Stob Cadha Gobhlach, *peak of the forked pass,* then north towards Corrag Bhuidhe Buttress. At the bealach, the route leaves An Teallach's spine to descend on steep grass into the southeastern corner of Coir' a' Ghamhna.

It is unlikely that there will be anyone else in this spectacular western corrie and it has an immediate feeling of intimacy. From just below the noise of wind and voices on the ridge, the corrie provides shelter and silence, its walls shrinking the mountain's space to a few hundred square metres. Here, tracks and terraces are made by goats, deer and the forces of climate. For a solitary walker, this is somewhere to be truly on one's own.

Walking alone reduces the complexity of interactions to just two relationships: the first with place, the second with oneself. The first

139

is outward – the main melody of the day, stimulated by sight and sound, terrain and seasons – live and in the present, occupied with choices of route and movements in the landscape. Thoughts and memories are transformed to here and now by what is happening along the way – peaks, clouds, deer, an orchid, pine stumps, rock faces – bringing the natural environment into the role of companion for the day.

As a consequence of being alone, greater awareness of the mountain develops and outward attention through each of the senses is more acute than when in a group. Without the micro culture created by others, a solo walker can become part of the mountain *as it is*, bringing minimal distortion to its character by their presence.

"Only by going alone in silence, without baggage, can one truly get into the heart of the wilderness. All other travel is mere dust and hotels and baggage and chatter."

John Muir,
naturalist and conservationist (1888)

The second relationship is inward, an underscore, coming to the surface where walking is easy and breathing even and steady. It may be a daydream, or a light trance-like state of mind, with sense of time and place suspended. As the body continues to walk the rhythm, the mind plays with deeper harmonies, ranging over past and future, reality and imagination, and visiting other contexts.

When preoccupations far removed from the mountains loom large in life, they clamour for attention whenever there is a vacant space. Temporarily, they may push the outward melody of crag, ridge and corrie aside and become companions on the mountain. Being

alone on steep ground and seeking a way down are immediate necessities that banish such thoughts and replace them with the need for balance, step by step choice and assessment of consequences. There is no one else in whose footmarks to follow and within a few seconds attention is claimed back to the present.

"... to be properly enjoyed a walking tour should be gone upon alone. If you go in company it is no longer a walking tour in anything but name. A walking tour should be gone upon alone because freedom is of the essence; because you should be able to stop and go on, and follow this way or that and because you must have your own pace."

Robert Louis Stevenson
novelist, essayist and travel writer
Walking Tours (1881)

The route moves downwards facing the stony northern crescent of Coir' a' Ghamhna and the sharp edge that falls from Sgurr Creag an Eich to its namesake crag. At the northwest is a sidelong perspective of Strathnashellag Forest, where An Teallach's slopes drop to a shelf of upland grazing then again to the shore of Loch na Sealga.

The lower half of the descent is beside a fence enclosing relics of woodland around the Allt a' Ghamhna. Posts and wire are the most obvious signs of human activity in the corrie, already showing success in giving protection to new growth of trees.

facing page: *Coir' a' Ghamhna*

140

Exclosure, Coir' a' Ghamhna

Larachantivore

Shenavall

Since the time when grinding ice cut Coir' a' Ghamhna from the side of An Teallach and gave Loch na Sealga its length and depth, no other forces as great have impinged on the mountain landscape. Subsequent changes have touched only the surface of the ground: forest has been and gone, as have large and wild animals, domestic crops and human communities.

Where the Allt a' Ghamhna enters the loch at An Teallach's southwestern foot, the route turns southeast to follow the old established highway, drove route and public right of way along Strath na Sealga for the next five kilometres. It goes past sites where people dwelt for centuries – Shenavall, Achneigie and across the rivers, Larachantivore – their genetic lineage rooted in the strath, to which came occasional new faces: Vikings from Scandinavia, drovers from Lewis and Harris, travellers with wares to sell, priests, military surveyors and map makers. Some may have stayed as settlers but by the nineteenth century all native people were gone, removed to the coast. Where boots tread now, thousands, perhaps hundreds of thousands, of feet have been before: the tread of hunter and woodsman; the tread of homecoming, cultivation and herding; the tread of travelling and trading; the tread of eviction, of new enterprise; now the tread of recreation and mountaineering. They walked this same way with An Teallach at their back, or lived with the mountain's timeless profile, bold and familiar, even from a distance. However far away its local people went, the image of An Teallach will have stayed with them in memory.

"Walking connects you to the land, it sews a seam between you and it that is very hard to unstitch."

Kelly Winters, long distance walker
Walking Home (2001)

On well-worn paths, necessity for moment by moment attention to the ground ahead is removed, making it possible to walk for hours without giving the outside world more than an occasional thought. This is a mixed blessing; it can provide time for thinking about the surroundings as an historic place, or equally, time for disconnecting from them. It can remove a hillwalker in all but body from strath or mountainside, and reduce their relationship with it to the touch of their soles. On a good track, attention is directed wherever the walker wishes, or where their needs are greatest.

Long distance trails, signposted and frequently used, give many days of reflection time. It is no wonder that for some of the people who walk them, the experience changes their lives. Outwardly, although the path is long, it is known; but inwardly the journey is much bigger, and may be full of unknowns. To the path or the place, the significance of one more passing pair of feet is not great; much greater is the significance of the path to the person.

For some, the desire to walk long distances is as much psychological as it is physical, historical, environmental or aesthetic. Prior to her walk on the Appalachian Trail (2,100 miles) Kelly Winters, an American novelist, wrote :

"Certainty grows in me that there's a place I need to get to – not a physical place, but an emotional, psychological, spiritual one. And although the place is not physical, somehow the only way to get there is to physically walk, a long, slow, arduous process. A pilgrimage. I don't know what that place is or what I'll find there, but I trust that it exists, it's reachable, and it's as necessary as blood or breath."

Kelly Winters
Walking Home (2001)

Descent to Strath na Sealga

Prolonged periods of walking, like running, jogging and other physical exercise, are known to have psychological benefits. Over two and a half thousand years ago, Hippocrates, physician in ancient Greece, said that walking was *'man's best medicine.'* Exercise increases the blood supply to the brain, stimulates the hormone system and improves mood, particularly through the production of endorphins – natural to the body, chemically close to opiates and with similar effects – providing a relaxed state of mind that is open to ideas. Many people return from a walk having sorted out their thoughts or made a decision; yet when this happens, they are unable to say exactly how or where it occurred. They may not have been aware that they were taking time to think about a difficult issue and its resolution may come as a surprise.

The mental state created by endorphins affects both conscious and unconscious processes and resembles a light therapeutic trance. The unconscious mind stores experiences, memories and thoughts, all of which can be combined and are available as roots for new concepts, creative ideas and solutions to problems.

Endorphins appear to help in making links between the unconscious and the conscious mind, giving insight and even inspiration. They are part of the exquisite mix that mountaineers treasure at summit moments, after hours of extreme effort and focus.

"... that blessed mood,
In which the burthen of the mystery,
In which the heavy and the weary weight
Of all this unintelligible world
Is lighten'd."

William Wordsworth
Lines composed a few miles above Tintern Abbey
(1798)

For someone who has been there, the experience of this route on An Teallach – across the moor by the lochans, high up on the crags and ridge, picking a way down through the corrie – will have already entered into a store of memory. It will be there to draw upon whenever it is needed: in future days on the mountains and as a resourceful metaphor for other times, when life requires the creation of an individual path, or there is no established way.

Ridge and corrie: Sail Liath (right), Stob Cadha Gobhlach (centre), the bealach and upper Coir' a' Ghamhna

Remnants of alder woodland beside the right of way in Strath na Sealga

Without being asked, the unconscious mind of a mountaineer connects An Teallach with other mountains in the person's past and future and with different parts of their life. In much the same way, while out for a long walk and experiencing that enjoyable state of day-dreaming, their unconscious mind is stimulated to get to work, and at any moment may come up with a solution to what has previously been absorbing their thoughts. Once found at an unconscious level, the solution is presented to the conscious mind, where it arrives amongst whatever else is going on, seemingly out of the blue.

Walking is recreation in its fundamental sense, meaning renewal and refreshment.

Mountaineers, climbers and hillwalkers have a relationship with mountains that trusts in the delight they will bring, and it is more than likely that they will also trust the results that the mountains provide for their relationship with self, in the form of a decision made or a complex issue unravelled. A hundred years ago John Muir (1838-1914) realised the effect that being amongst mountains and the natural world had on his inner state, and wrote in his journal:

"I only went out for a walk and finally concluded to stay out till sundown, for going out, I found, was really going in."

John of the Mountains.
The Unpublished Journals of John Muir

Between two World Wars, when mountaineering was beginning to be accessible to a wider range of people and the 1932 Kinder Trespass had begun the fight for the right to roam, Frank Smythe, British mountaineer and pacifist, wrote *The Spirit of the Hills*. He described experiences of being in the mountains with similar passion to John Muir, combining physical, mental and spiritual aspects, and he knew that a day in the hills offered freedom of thought which could put a different perspective on the stresses of city life. His wish was that other human beings should *'seek an inspiration and solace for self-made muddles in the simplicity and quietude of Nature.'* (Smythe, 1934)

"Climb the mountains and get their good tidings. Nature's peace will flow into you as sunshine flows into trees. The winds will blow their own freshness into you, and the storms their energy, while cares will drop off like autumn leaves."

John Muir (1901)

Where Strath na Sealga narrows and the drove route goes south by Loch an Nid, the track begins to rise, looping back up the hillside with the winding river below and the view turned towards An Teallach again. Inward attention is sparked outward; splashes of gold from flowering gorse brighten the browns of late winter and early spring; the head of Loch na Sealga is in the distance; the southern quarter of the mountain is in front.

As the track climbs higher, the route leaves it. The exact point of departure is an individual choice and the final part of the route returns to the start, over the moor with its dozens of lochans. If the track is left as soon as it reaches 300 metres, the line of walking is a new one, going northeast with An Teallach in sight at the northwest; or leaving the track later, the route is similar to earlier in the day but in reverse, with the mountain behind.

"The more I climbed that day, the more I grew besotted with the whole mountain, not with its summits and serrations and ridgey intricacies (and certainly not with the view from the top because there is nothing in that vast all-around panorama which compares to the mountain where you stand, and which you cannot see because you are standing on it), but with the whole stockpiled scope of the mountain."

Jim Crumley, mountaineer
Among Mountains (1993)

Approaching the last few hundred metres, the near horizon is almost featureless and the telecommunications mast is hidden below the edge of the moorland. Close sight of mast and road – symbolic of technology and present day connection with others – comes only at the very end of the route.

Before leaving the open ground, turn once more towards the great mountain. Remember the experience of being there, of touching its rock, exploring its rarely trodden places and adding your footprints to the paths of its history; and now, make a place in memory for An Teallach, *the forge*.

"No matter how well you get to know the Scottish Highlands, no matter how often you have glimpsed a particular scene, this tremendously varied area seems forever to retain its power to impose itself, all of a sudden, on your mind."

James Hunter, historian
On the Other Side of Sorrow (1995)

facing page:
Toll an Lochain seen across An Teallach's eastern moorland

146

REFERENCES &
SELECT BIBLIOGRAPHY

REFERENCES

References, including sources of quotations, are listed by chapter, in the order in which they appear in the text.

1. INTRODUCTION

Ralph Storer, from *100 Best Routes on Scottish Mountains* (David & Charles, 1987)

W. H. Murray, from *Undiscovered Scotland* (J. M. Dent & Sons Ltd, 1951)

Mike Cawthorne, from *Hell of a journey: On foot through the Scottish Highlands in winter* (Mercat Press, 2000)

Thomas Pennant, from *A Tour in Scotland and Voyage to the Hebrides 1772* (John Monk, Chester, 1774 Part 1, 1776 Part 2; reprinted by Birlinn Ltd, 1998)

Seton Gordon, from *Highways and Byways in the West Highlands* (MacMillan & Co Ltd, 1935; reprinted by Birlinn Ltd, 1995)

Simon Schama, from *Landscape and Memory* (Harper Collins Publishers, 1996)

James Hunter, from *Last of the Free* (Mainstream Publishing Company Ltd, 1999)

2. WINTER

W. H. Murray, from *Undiscovered Scotland* (J. M. Dent & Sons Ltd, 1951)

John Muir, from *My First Summer in the Sierra* (Houghton, Mifflin & Company, 1911)

Carl Sagan, from *The Cosmic Connection: an Extraterrestial Perspective* (Anchor Press/Doubleday, 1973)

W. H. Murray, from *Undiscovered Scotland* (J. M. Dent & Sons, 1951)

Thomas Pennant, from *A Tour in Scotland and Voyage to the Hebrides 1772* (John Monk, Chester, 1774 Part 1, 1776 Part 2; reprinted by Birlinn Ltd, 1998)

John MacCulloch from *The Highlands and Western Islands of Scotland,* Vol. II (1824), in Ian Mitchell, *Scotland's Mountains before the Mountaineers* (Luath Press Ltd, 1998)

W. W. King and H.T. Munro from *An Teallach: Ross-shire* (Scottish Mountaineering Club Journal, Vol. III, 1893)

W. H. Murray, from *Undiscovered Scotland* (J. M. Dent & Sons, 1951)

Seton Gordon, from *Highways and Byways in the West Highlands* (MacMillan & Co Ltd, 1935; reprinted by Birlinn Ltd, 1995)

facing page: An Teallach from the west (October)

3. SPRING

Seton Gordon, from *Highways and Byways in the West Highlands* (MacMillan & Co Ltd, 1935; reprinted by Birlinn Ltd, 1995)

W. A. Poucher, from *The Scottish Peaks* (Constable & Company, 1965)

Cameron McNeish, from *The Munros, Scotland's Highest Mountains* (Lomond Books, 1996)

Clarrie Pashley and Martin Moran, from *The Magic of Wester Ross and Skye* (David & Charles, 2001)

Chris Drury, from *The edge is the division* (1995), in *Found Moments in Time and Space* (Harry N. Abrams, Inc., 1998)

4. SUMMER

Moray McLaren, from *The Scots* (Penguin Books, 1951)

Raymond Eagle, from *Introduction* in Seton Gordon, *Highways and Byways in the West Highlands* (Birlinn Ltd, 1995)

Maria Coffey, from *Where the mountain casts its shadow* (Hutchinson, 2003)

John Muir, from *My First Summer in the Sierra* (Houghton, Mifflin & Company, 1911)

William Wordsworth, from *Lines composed a few miles above Tintern Abbey* (1798)

William Blake (1757-1827), from *Auguries of Innocence*

Alan Gussow, from *A Sense of Place* (Friends of the Earth, 1972)

5. AUTUMN

James Hunter, from *Last of the Free* (Mainstream Publishing Company Ltd, 1999)

Gaelic poem translation in James Hunter, *On the Other Side of Sorrow* (Mainstream Publishing Company Ltd, 1995)

Gavin Maxwell, from *Ring of Bright Water* (Longmans, Green & Co Ltd, 1960)

Geoff Cohen, from *Northern Highlands* (Scottish Mountaineering Trust, 1993)

6. PLACE

Clarrie Pashley and Martin Moran, from *The Magic of Wester Ross and Skye* (David & Charles, 2001)

Henry David Thoreau from *The Writings of Henry David Thoreau* (1906) in Joseph Cornell, *Listening to Nature* (Exley Publications Ltd, 1987)

John Muir, from *My First Summer in the Sierra* (Houghton, Mifflin & Company, 1911)

Julian Huxley, from *Preface* in Rachel Carson, *Silent Spring* (Hamish Hamilton, 1963)

James Hunter, from *On the Other Side of Sorrow* (Mainstream Publishing Company Ltd, 1995)

Joseph Cornell, from *Listening to Nature* (Exley Publications Ltd, 1987)

Robert Pirsig, from *Zen and the Art of Motorcycle Maintenance* (William Morrow & Company, 1974)

Alan Gussow, from *A Sense of Place* (Friends of the Earth, 1972)

Jim Crumley, from *Among Mountains* (Mainstream Publishing Company Ltd, 1993)

Robert M. Pirsig, from *Zen and the Art of Motorcycle Maintenance* (William Morrow & Company, 1974)

7. SUMMIT

John MacCulloch, from *Highlands and Western Isles,* Vol. II (1824) in W. W. King and H. T. Munro, *An Teallach: Ross-shire* (Scottish Mountaineering Club Journal, Vol. III, 1893)

Leslie Stephen, from *The Playgrounds of Europe* (Longman, 1894)

F. S. Smythe, from *The Spirit of the Hills* (Hodder & Stoughton, 1935)

Richard Gilbert, from *Lonely Hills and Wilderness Trails* (David & Charles, 2000)

John MacCulloch, from *Highlands and Western Isles,* Vol. II (1824) in W. W. King and H. T. Munro, *An Teallach: Ross-shire* (Scottish Mountaineering Club Journal, Vol. III, 1893)

Compton Mackenzie, from *Shiant Islands, text of a radio talk* (1928) in Douglas Dunn (ed.), *Scotland, An Anthology* (Harper Collins, 1991)

8. TIME

James Hunter, from *On the Other Side of Sorrow* (Mainstream Publishing Company Ltd, 1995)

Jane Jacobs, from *The Death and Life of Great American Cities* (Random House, 1961; reprinted by Pelican Books, 1965)

Wendell Berry, from *Preserving Wildness* in *Home Economics, Fourteen Essays* (North Point Press, 1987)

James Hunter, from *On the Other Side of Sorrow* (Mainstream Publishing Company Ltd, 1995)

Neil M. Gunn, from Alistair McCleery (ed.) *Landscape and Light, Essays by Neil M. Gunn* (Aberdeen University Press, 1987)

James Hunter, from *Last of the Free* (Mainstream Publishing Company Ltd, 1999)

9. RIDGE

Ralph Storer, from *100 Best Routes on Scottish Mountains* (David & Charles, 1987)

W. W. King and H. T. Munro from *An Teallach: Ross-shire* (Scottish Mountaineering Club Journal, Vol. III, 1893)

Linnie Marshe Wolfe from *Son to the Wilderness: A Life of John Muir* (Alfred A. Knopf, 1945)

W. W. King and H. T. Munro from *An Teallach: Ross-shire* (Scottish Mountaineering Club Journal, Vol. III, 1893)

Cameron McNeish, from *The Munros, Scotland's Highest Mountains* (Lomond Books, 1996)

10. CONNECTION

J. R. L. Anderson and Fay Godwin, from *The Oldest Road, An Exploration of the Ridgeway* (Whittet Books, 1975)

John MacCulloch, from *Highlands and Western Isles,* Vol. II (1824) in W. W. King and H. T. Munro, *An Teallach: Ross-shire* (Scottish Mountaineering Club Journal, Vol. III, 1893)

Jim Crumley, from *Among Mountains* (Mainstream Publishing Company Ltd, 1993)

A. F. Mummery, from *My Climbs in the Alps and Caucasus* (Fisher & Unwin, 1895)

John Muir, from *Letter to wife Louie, July 1888*, in *Life and Letters of John Muir* (Houghton, Mifflin & Company, 1924)

Robert Louis Stevenson, from *Walking Tours* in *Virginibus Puerisque and Other Papers* (Kegan Paul, 1881)

Jim Crumley, from *Among Mountains* (Mainstream Publishing Company Ltd, 1993)

Kelly Winters, from *Walking Home. A Woman's Pilgrimage on the Appalachian Trail* (Alyson Books, 2001)

William Wordsworth, from *Lines composed a few miles above Tintern Abbey* (1798)

John Muir, from *John of the Mountains, The Unpublished Journals of John Muir*. Linnie Marshe Wolfe (ed.) (Madison: University of Wisconsin Press, 1938; republished 1979)

F. S. Smythe, from *The Spirit of the Hills* (Hodder & Stoughton Limited, 1934)

John Muir, from *Our National Parks* (Houghton, Mifflin & Company, 1901)

Jim Crumley, from *Among Mountains* (Mainstream Publishing Company Ltd, 1993)

James Hunter, from *On the Other Side of Sorrow* (Mainstream Publishing Company Ltd, 1995)

SELECT BIBLIOGRAPHY

Alston, David (1999) *Ross and Cromarty, A Historical Guide* (Birlinn Ltd)

Baldwin, John R. (ed.) (1986) *Firthlands of Ross and Sutherland* (The Scottish Society for Northern Studies)

Baldwin, John R. (ed.) (1994) *Peoples and settlement in North-west Ross* (The Scottish Society for Northern Studies)

Bartholomew, J. C., D. J. Bennet and C. Stone (1995, 3rd revised edition) *Scottish Hill Tracks, A guide to hill paths, old roads and rights of way* (The Scottish Rights of Way Society and The Scottish Mountaineering Trust)

Bennet, Donald J. & Tom Strang (1990) *The Northwest Highlands* (The Scottish Mountaineering Trust)

Bennet, Donald J. (ed.) *The Munros* (1991, 2nd edition)(The Scottish Mountaineering Trust)

Brondsted, Johannes (1960) *The Vikings* (Penguin Books Ltd)

Campbell, Robin N. (1999) *The Munroist's Companion* (The Scottish Mountaineering Trust)

Coffey, Maria (2003) *Where the mountain casts its shadow* (Hutchinson)

Cohen, Geoff (1993) *Northern Highlands Rock and Ice Climbs Volume 1, Knoydart to An Teallach* (The Scottish Mountaineering Trust)

Crumley, Jim (1993) *Among Mountains* (Mainstream Publishing Company Ltd)

Csikszentmihalyi, Mihaly (1990) *Flow: The Psychology of Optimal Experience* (Harper & Row)

Dixon, J. H. (1886, reprinted 1980) *Gairloch and Guide to Loch Maree* (1886, Co-operative Printing Company, Edinburgh) (1980, Gairloch & District Heritage Society)

Drummond, Peter (1991) *Scottish Hill and Mountain Names* (The Scottish Mountaineering Trust)

Drury, Chris (1998) *Found Moments in Time and Space* (Harry N. Abrams, Inc.)

Gilbert, Richard (2000) *Lonely Hills and Wilderness Trails* (David & Charles)

Gordon, Seton (1935) (reprinted 1995) *Highways and Byways in the West Highlands* (1935, MacMillan & Co Ltd) (1995, Birlinn Ltd)

Grant, I. F. (1961) *Highland Folk Ways* (1980 edition) (Routledge & Kegan Paul Ltd)

Haldane, A. R. B. (1997) *The Drove Roads of Scotland* (Birlinn Ltd)

Hunter, James (1995) *On the Other Side of Sorrow* (Mainstream Publishing Company Ltd)

Hunter, James (1999) *Last of the Free* (Mainstream Publishing Company Ltd)

Mabey, Richard (ed.) (1997) *The Oxford Book of Nature Writing* (Oxford University Press)

Mackenzie, Osgood (1921) *A Hundred Years in the Highlands* (1980 reprint) (The National Trust for Scotland)

Maxwell, Gavin (1960) *Ring of Bright Water* (Longmans, Green & Co Ltd)

Mitchell, Ian (1998) *Scotland's Mountains before the Mountaineers* (Luath Press Ltd)

McNeish, Cameron (1996) *The Munros, Scotland's Highest Mountains* (Lomond Books)

Murray, W. H. (1951) *Undiscovered Scotland* (J. M. Dent & Sons Ltd)

Nicholson, Angela (1993) *The Complete Traveller's Guide to Gairloch and Torridon* (Thistle Press)

Omand, Donald (ed.) (1984) *The Ross and Cromarty Book* (The Northern Times Ltd)

Ordnance Survey (1981) *Place names on maps of Scotland and Wales* (Director General of the Ordnance Survey)

Pennant, Thomas *A Tour in Scotland and Voyage to the Hebrides 1772* (John Monk, Chester, 1774 Part 1, 1776 Part 2; reprinted by Birlinn Ltd, 1998)

Pirsig, Robert (1974) *Zen and the Art of Motorcycle Maintenance* (William Morrow & Company)

Poucher, W. A. (7th edition 1988) *The Scottish Peaks* (Constable & Company Ltd)

Schama, Simon (1996) *Landscape and Memory* (Harper Collins Publishers)

Storer, Ralph (1987)(1997*) *100 Best Routes in Scottish Mountains* (David & Charles) (*Warner Books, London)

Uncles, Christopher J. (1999) *Old Ways through Wester Ross* (Stenlake Publishing)

van Matre, Steve, and Bill Weiler (ed.) (1983) *The Earth Speaks* (The Institute for Earth Education)

Watson, W. J. (1904) (reprinted 1976) *Place-names of Ross and Cromarty* (Ross & Cromarty Heritage Society)

Willis, Douglas (1991) *The Story of Crofting in Scotland* (John Donald Publishers Ltd)

Wormell, Peter (2003) *Pinewoods of the Black Mount* (Dalesman Publishing Co Ltd)

overleaf: *An Teallach from the west (January)*

INDEX

Page numbers in *italics* denote photographs

facing page & rear cover:
An Teallach from the west (December sunrise)

"What a mountain!"

overheard on Sgurr Fiona
25th June 2004